First printing 2024

ISBN: 978-1-7398622-2-0

Wickham Publishing

wickhampublishing@yahoo.com

To my beautiful children, Caitlyn and Alex, who appear to be part of an experiment to show that mothers do not need sleep to survive, and my fantastic husband, who supports me in every way, who doesn't roll his eyes (too hard) when I add another dog to the household, or come up with outlandish ideas at 3am, like publishing a book.

The Parenting Diaries

The story that unfolds in the following pages is a tale of long nights, nappies, and a Small Child at war with sleep. In short, it is a foray into the life of a husband and wife who are taking on the greatest challenge of all... Parenting.

The key players in this saga are:

Me, myself, a 33 year old first time mother, who had an optimistic outlook, some great ideas and a very naive delight in the possibilities that lay ahead.

My husband, a 34 year old first time father, who didn't have a clue what he was getting into, and only really had inkling when he realised our daughter would be just like me.

Various four legged financial burdens, all of the canine variety. Some are delighted with the addition of a Small Child to their midst, and one definitely is not.

And of course, the star of the show, Small Child herself. Our first child, who, from day one, has had very strong opinions about life, and her place in it. The crux of the matter, as many first time parents can attest, is that Small Child's opinions and beliefs do not always align with those of her parents, especially when it comes to sleep.

These diaries are the product of many a sleepless night, one too many cups of tea, and several packets of hobnobs. If you recognise yourself or your family in these pages, I can only apologise, I think I ate all the biscuits already. I have also started on the gin.

Sit back and read on. It might just feel very familiar.

DAY The First (Or, Who's Bright Idea Was This Anyway?)

Gentle reader we have embarked upon a wondrous journey into parenthood.

So, we shall begin.

At some point yesterday, those in charge declared that both I and the other inmate were technically functioning adults and therefore were responsible for this small child. After hastily pointing out that we were really just winging it, some friendly native pointed out that a baby is nothing more than a houseplant with emotions. Keep em fed, watered and make sure they get sunlight. Sounds simple? That's all well and good until you realise that between us we are yet to keep a houseplant alive for more than a few weeks.

Having been sent forth, whilst clutching said Small Child, we found ourselves sitting, if not quite upon a peak in Darien, then at least upon a sofa in Groesffordd, showing the required wild surmise whist staring at each other. Apparently small children don't come with manuals. We actually have to figure this out on the fly.

We are no strangers to winging it, in fact, we have turned it into an art form. The addition of a Small Child into our midst just means that we need to at least look like we know what we're doing.

Gentle reader, if you wish to see how this plays out, read on. I suspect it'll be worth a chuckle or two.

DAY The Second (or So Far, So Good)

Gentle reader, we have survived the first test, and made it through 24 hours. Slightly over in fact. There have been three poos. One, a surprise event. Not only did Small Child manage to wait until Daddy had successfully cleaned up the first, she waited for the opportune moment in his halfway celebrations to present him with a second. Both hands full, legs in the air (the former being his, the latter hers) not a nappy to be seen. If nothing else this will teach him to wait until all behinds are secure before starting the victory lap.

As I speak, the face of innocence is passed out in my arms. It is apparently exhausting being adorable, and she requires rest from her terrible exertions. I suspect this desire for sleep will long continue, as a direct result of carrying all the looks, charisma and humour in the family. I should know, it has been my burden for these many years.

Our canine companions have declared their verdict on the newest member of the household. It is almost unanimous that she has been accepted, with open paws. Our sticking point however, is Hope. She has decreed that as peasants go, it's a relatively small one, and it makes little to no noise. This is acceptable. On the other hand, it is a peasant. It was brought in with no consultation and without proper clearance. The fact we were talking about it for the past nine months is neither here nor there. And in the grand scheme of things, here is not the option she would have voted for.

DAY The Third (or, Does This Child Have Hollow Legs?)

Gentle reader, we have successfully completed another day without serious mishap. This is starting to feel like the safety level of a computer game, life is going rather too well, we've mastered the controls and bested one or two baddies. Clearly we now feel invincible. So naturally I'm facing the immediate future with the confidence of a four year old on a brand new push bike, who has no idea yet that some helpful person has removed their training wheels.

Today saw the return of my appetite for the first time in weeks. If it stood still, I wanted to eat it. If it was moving, I sent the other inmate to shoot it and cook it for it's audacity. Upon observation of this, Small Child also took the Eat, Drink and Be Merry view of things, and in those moments where she was awake, drank what can only be described as the liquid equivalent of Belgium. At each sitting.

Daddy is yet to learn that his daughter is made in the same mould as Zeeva. If they are awake, they're hungry. If they're asleep, don't mention food. Or if you do, you had best be prepared to follow up on that idea, pronto. While we are so far, blessed with a child who doesn't cry, I am absolutely sure that if we spoke baby, she already knows some words that would shock her grandparents. There may be no snooze button on a Schnauzer wanting breakfast, but equally there is no mute button on a Small Child who has just heard the word lunch.

DAY The Fourth (or, My Dog Is Judging My Parenting Skills)

Gentle reader, now is the time to introduce you to the other members of the household. A group collectively known as the Four Legged Financial Burdens. Also known as A Very Expensive Life Decision, or How To Test Your Marriage Vows On A Regular Basis. In other words, we pay the mortgage so a motley crew of schnauzers can take over the best spot on the sofa, and ensure the local vet can afford several luxury holidays a year. We currently act like we can control five of the little delights, and so you can understand the full range of our family dynamics, a quick run through is essential.

We have Huzzah, the elder statesman. The most loving Beard ever to woof at a postman, he has now discovered a calling as a bodyguard for the Small Child.

Grandma Kaegen is up next. Large, loving and 100% would help you rob the place if you had chicken.

Hope. Does Not Play Well With Others. She nurses a high level of disdain for the human race. While she would never hurt a fly, this is not wholly due to the goodness of her heart, but more so because savaging someone's trouser legs would involve her having to touch them. And she would not do that if you paid her.

Zeeva, an angel on four legs, she is sunshine personified. It is impossible not to love her. She has been the Mother Bear of our gang; she has raised 13 puppies, and is the happiest soul in the world.

Gatland. Chaos is his middle name, and Loki is his half brother (no, really. Some poor soul actually has to deal with him. And oh boy was he aptly named). Zeeva's son, who I apologise to her daily for keeping.

So there you have it. The selection of characters with which we share this happy abode. Today, I discovered that while I may view them in a positive, happy light, this may not always be reciprocated. Well obviously! I hear you cry with impatience. We've met Hope. We know that humanity is a far cry from what she deems to be on the borders of acceptable. Oh Gentle reader, while right in essentials, it pains me to tell you how wrong you are. I have indeed been relegated to the Peasant List for many years. I have made my peace with that. Today, I became aware that another has judged me, and found me wanting. And the realisation rocked me to my very core.

It is Zeeva.

Recover yourselves. Take a moment. There are smelling salts available in the foyer.

Yes, I am now fully aware that Little Miss Sunshine has spent the last few days observing, scoring and shaking her head at my parenting skills, or lack thereof. Today, she delivered her verdict, and it was damning. She, having raised 13 small beards, feels that she is somewhat of an expert. I don't dispute her claim, however I have pointed out that her life choices and mine are very different. This however has not stopped her berating me for not treating Small Child like Poppy 14. How dare I put her down? How very dare I not clean her ears. And as if I actually let just anyone pick her up. Every move I make is accompanied by a glare, dire muttering, and quite often a swift paw to the leg or eye. I am under the impression that I am receiving strict parenting lessons, and I am not sure she is impressed with my progress.

I haven't the heart to tell her that I don't need worming next week. I think she is looking forward to that.

DAY The Fifth (Or We Already Need More Space)

Gentle reader, it is a well established fact that some women like clothes. It is, usually, an interest that develops over time, and generally results in the need for additional storage. Friends, let me tell you, in the space of five short days, this Small Child has amassed so many outfits, that it is entirely possible we need, if not a new house, then at least an extension. I am confident that she owns more outfits than me, and also that she is more stylish. It is both impressive and chastening.

In other news, this epistle comes to you rather later than normal, for last night the other inmate, henceforth known as Daddy, took charge of the night feeds. Gentle reader, it was glorious. For when you have prior knowledge of the 1am poo that awaits, you take great pleasure in watching someone else approach these moments with equal measure of naivety and delight.

It did not disappoint.

DAY The Sixth (Or, I Now Deserve All The Wine)

Gentle reader, today saw a milestone in my recovery process. We had the removal of the dressing.

Now, for some reason, known only to the sadist that put the damn thing on, the positioning of said dressing meant that I had become an unwilling volunteer for an at home bikini wax.

One can only assume that it was applied by a man. Its removal involved a rather brave midwife, wine, and a husband who came within inches of experiencing his own mystery wax appointment (note, never laugh at your wife having a dressing removed, especially when she is between you and the only safe escape route. Certainly never laugh twice).

While the end result is almost what we would desire, and despite me currently looking like a multi coloured, colour blind Picasso wannabe around the midriff, I am struggling to believe that Small Child made their entrance through such a small exit. Personally I think she came out flat-packed. Either way, just thinking about it is enough to drive me to drink. And in this house, that's never a very long drive.

One thing is for certain however. Those of you who voluntarily wax anything are certifiable. Those of you who do it without wine, we can't be friends.

DAY The Seventh (Or, We Survived A Week)

Gentle reader, a milestone, a rather important one, has been reached. It has been a whole seven days and frankly, we're both still standing. I'd look shocked too.

Obviously, this is testament to the fact we have spent our whole lives practicing for this very event. And by practicing, I mean we have been winging just about everything, and people still believe we are functioning adults.

No great dramas engulfed our day, unless you count strategic weeing on a basket of freshly washed, about to go on the line, white baby gros. Thank you Gatland. I did not count it as any momentous event, but he is lucky to still have his testicles.

The other inmate was tentatively approached regarding football on the morrow. He declined in haste, citing wife issues, of which he has plenty. Having seen the weather this morning, he owes me one. And by one, I mean a packet of jammy dodgers. It is only fitting.

The focus of our weekend is to ensure that we have enough wine, and I am absolutely convinced someone mentioned cheesecake. If they didn't, they should.

DAY The Eighth (Or, Disney Lied To Me And Now I'm Confused)

Gentle reader, having spent parts of last eight days singing and rocking this Small Child, I decided, somewhat rashly, to add bedtime fairy tales to our repertoire.

I see you all smiling fondly, thinking, what could be a more perfectly maternal picture. And in essence oh Gentle reader, I agree. On the facts however, things are markedly different, and I am shook.

Picture, if you will. A Peter Rabbit themed nursery, with midnight blue curtains, decorated with silver stars. A rocking chair, complete with mother and baby in the corner, watched over by a vintage teddy bear. A perfectly crocheted rainbow blanket, tucked around a sleepy baby, a schnauzer and a large book of fairy tales resting on mother's knee. Idyllic, no?

Gentle reader, tonight we read The Little Mermaid. The night before, Pinocchio. Delightful, whimsical fairy tales. I remember them well from my childhood obsession with Disney.

Now, the only time Disney has ever given me unrealistic years expectations, was about the number of dogs I could own, the willingness of local animals to help with the housework, the availability and convenient location of any number of handsome princes, and the ability to fix any situation with a song. Minor details.

Until now.

Disney Lied. The little Mermaid is not a gentle, romantic, girl meets boy, boy has dog, girl has fish, they all lived happily ever after love story. It's dark, twisted, she tries to murder people and she dies. Not *exactly* how Disney portrayed it. And the worst betrayal? She's blonde. It shook me to my very core. And friends, Pinocchio is not much better.

I am staring at the title page of Hansel and Gretel. I assumed before this that I knew the content. I may be wrong. I am not brave enough to find out.

Is it too early for gin?

DAY The Ninth, (Or, She can't focus but oh boy can she aim)

Gentle reader, today has been glorious, for many reasons. Today we have had both firsts, and events of note. Sit down dear friends, and enjoy.

Our day started well, Small Child was impeccably behaved and slept until a civilised hour. She even had the good grace not to cry when having a nappy change. She was, in short, a delight. Fast forward around two hours. Enter Daddy. Daddy has been remarkable this week, often being found in the midst of the battle, brandishing a nappy or several. Not a man to be taken down lightly. Until today.

Having handed parental responsibility to said father figure for what seemed, to all intents and purposes, a straight forward nappy change, I took the opportunity to live decadently, and indulge in a sneaky biscuit. I have barely licked the evidence from my fingers, when a plaintive voice is heard from above, requesting immediate assistance. In a manner that did not call to mind a fleet of foot gazelle (think more along the lines of a three legged, rather chunky elephant. Definitely built for feed, not speed), I leapt to my feet and ascended, like a ministering angel. The sight that met my eyes was this. A happy, naked and gurgling baby on the changing table, with her loving daddy bent over attentively. A picture of domestic bliss, if you will

Then Daddy turned round.

Gentle reader, our child can vomit. Her aim is impeccable. She not only got it in his ear, but down the front of his shirt, and inside the collar. She covered all angles, quite literally. Obviously my response was to rush in, rescue my beloved husband and clean, making sure all parties were well...

After I finished laughing and could let go of the bannister.

She may not be able to focus, but dear lord this child can aim to perfection, and her level of unconcern post event was legendary. I'm proud of her.

DAY The Tenth (or, I Can Now See My Legs Again)

Gentle reader, today I have rejoiced. Loudly and without hesitation, for today's achievement was mine, and mine alone.

It may interest you to know, that prior to the arrival of this Small Child, I was instructed to don the most fetching stockings. I see some of you nodding sagely in the wings, no doubt recalling your own run ins with these delightful accoutrements. To add insult to injury, these were also bottle green. I can manage most things, but having spent my carefree youth in a school uniform of that particular shade, this was an uncomfortable reminder that nothing good ever came in bottle green.

Following the arrival of Small Child, and after all the obligatory questions (are you sure she is a girl? Does she come with instructions? Does she need a kennel name? You know, the usuals), my follow up, and possibly more vital question was regarding the duration of my torture. To whit, precisely how long will these fetching stockings be a part of my life?

I'm fairly sure they heard my wild cry of despair back home when some well meaning soul mentioned ten days.

Friends, I have been suffering. My very soul has been harrowed. For ten days, nights included, I have paraded round with bottle green legs and feet. My toes have stuck out at inconvenient times. Comfort has not been a word we have used. It has not been pleasant. I almost preferred the injections that have come alongside. At least that pain was fleeting. The fashion faux pas has been permanent.

And then, Day Ten. Oh what joy! What relief! I can feel the air. I can look down, and I have never been so pleased to be compared to Casper in my life. My legs have returned to me.

Gentle reader, we have now but one problem. I still can't bend. And after ten days in solitary confinement, they need attention. And fast.

While my leg based troubles may not yet be over, I can for now rejoice that I am no longer green. It's a small win, but we'll take it.

DAY The Eleventh (or The Day I Got All The Details Wrong)

Gentle reader, it is possible that at times, I get things wrong. Or at very least, I may provide details that are slightly, out. If we cast our minds back to the rehearsal for our wedding, both self and other inmate aged ourselves twelve months, by spectacularly forgetting our own dates of birth. Equally. I somehow missed two whole years of my nephew's life, and wished him a happy fifth birthday, when in fact he was seven. Repeat that in public, and I will deny all knowledge of course.

This brings us to two weeks ago. I may have altered Austin's date of birth when we attended for our Covid tests. I may have aged him slightly. We laughed. He corrected it. The nurse was amused.

Yesterday. Ah yes. The day we registered this Small Child. A day on which I realistically needed to be on the ball.

Was I? Was I hell.

A simple form to fill in, requiring, yet again, the date of birth for the other inmate. Did I recall the debacle of two weeks ago? Yes. Was I absolutely confident that I had learnt from such mistakes, and now knew, without a doubt when he was born? Definitely. Did I proceed to then get it wrong? Of course I did. I'm sure Austin is starting to wonder if fatherhood has aged him, or if I am advancing him into an early grave for the life insurance.

Gentle reader, I wish I could say that this was my only faux pas of the day. Alas, it was not to be. During the registration of the Small Child, not only did I divorce myself from the other inmate, and proudly announced my original surname, I also threw the date of our wedding into the wind. Even Small Child was unimpressed.

DAY The Twelfth (Or Today You Are Clean And Sweet Smelling)

Gentle reader, the time has come. Small Child had a bath. A momentous occasion. Partly for the photo opportunity in an adorable towel, partly because I wanted to see Daddy deal with a slippery, wiggly child. I've seen him bath Gatland, this can only be on a par with that. And Gatland was vaguely cooperative.

Having been told numerous times that Small Child will absolutely hate the bath, and will cry, we went in prepared. Wars have been less planned than this. We had swing music. Bubbles. A heat sensing duck. In true Hitchhiker's style, we even knew where our towels were. What we forgot Gentle reader, is that Small Child is contrary.

The look of wonderment as her bottom sank into warm water. The big wide eyes as she splashed about. The complete and utter silence with which she accepted soap and shampoo. Not a single cry escaped the bathroom.

Rashly, I suggested a bottle and bed to follow, because we all know bath time makes them sleepy.

Remind yourselves, if you will, of Small Child's personality. Sleepy is not a word we will be using post bath for quite some time.

To sum up. Baths are good. Shampoo is good. Baby bubbles are good.

Moisturiser on the other hand, is the devil's work.

DAY The Thirteenth (Or, The Day I Thought About Installing A Cow)

Gentle reader, as I write this latest missive, I am in need of coffee. I don't drink coffee as a rule, but at this time in the morning, and with the audience I have, it is probably more socially acceptable than gin.

Why then, I hear you cry, are you searching for a cup, given that you don't drink the stuff?

The answer is simple my friends. Growth. Spurt. Small Child has discovered that she is growing. And to do this, she requires copious amounts of milk, at regular intervals. Clearly when she wakes, it has been years since she was last fed, and she makes this known to us, loudly. I hesitate to suggest that she is a Diva or that, at two weeks old, she has already perfected the art of exaggeration, but gentle reader, I suspect it may be close to the truth.

I must run. Silence currently reigns, which can only mean one thing. Small Child is about to be hungry again. I must either prepare another feed, take out shares in SMA, or buy a cow.

DAY Friday The Thirteenth (Or, The Day Mummy Got Caught By The Halfway Poo)

Gentle reader, it has been 14 days since Small Child came into our world. In that time, I have heard tales from Daddy of an experience so harrowing that it has affected his whole week. It has become known as the Halfway Poo.

The first time Daddy experienced the phenomenon, I laughed. I laughed hard. The second time, I heaved a sigh of relief, as I had only handed off Small Child moments earlier.

Gentle reader, I have successfully avoided any and all involvement with said poo.

Until today.

Today, while I bravely did battle with the business end of Small Child, I was aware, halfway through, of a sudden silent stillness. The eye of the storm, if you will. In that moment, I knew.

The frantic grab for a nappy. The one handed bottom swivel away from my general direction. The expletive laden comments about Daddy shirking his duty. I had fallen foul (pun absolutely intended) of the Halfway Poo.

I am traumatised. My life shall never be the same again. Gentle reader, the moral of this story?

Silence during a nappy change is not golden. It's suspicious.

DAY The Fifteenth (Or Naked Baby Is A Dangerous Game To Play)

Gentle reader, you will be pleased to note that I have recovered from the trauma recounted in my last missive. It is truly amazing what a cup of tea will do for a harrowed soul.

Today however saw me dice with death, or at least, if not death, then with the very great possibility of needing to clean the carpet. Bravely, or rashly (the line is a fine one), while Daddy was running a bath and I was getting Small Child up from bed, I decided that putting a fresh nappy on would be a waste.

I know what you're thinking. Did I learn nothing from yesterday? Am I generally this reckless and devil may care? The answer to both, is no.

Round One.
I carried Small Child successfully across our cream carpets. We entered the bathroom and stood for a while, naked and free, while Daddy ran the final part of the bath, and warned me that I was playing a version of Russian Roulette that he would not advise so early in the morning.

I laughed, airily. Small Child also gurgled in what I can only describe as a dismissive tone. Daddy was worrying over nothing. Small Child was successfully plonked into the bath without incident.

Mummy 1. Small Child 0.

In hindsight Gentle reader, I should have quit while I was ahead.

Round Two.
Wrapped in a towel, Small Child was warm, dry and hungry. I sat her upon my lap and proceeded to apply a bottle industriously.

Daddy uttered a dire warning as he headed for the stairs. I may have attempted a second airy laugh, which was cut short in dramatic fashion as I became aware of warmth spreading along my leggings.

Mummy 1. Small Child 1.

While it is not physically possible at present, I swear she winked. This tells me one thing. The war has begun.

DAY The Sixteenth (Or, The Day I Threatened To Call Grandma)

Gentle reader, forgive me for the lateness of this missive. I know you have all been on tenterhooks, waiting desperately for the latest instalment. It is late, because of its contents. Much like Small Child's bedtime, the story of which I will now relate.

So far, Small Child has been angelic. The mere suggestion of bedtime for the adults (and I use that term loosely) at 9pm, and she plonks expectantly in my lap for a story, a song and away we go.

Rashly I spoke of now bringing her bedtime to 8pm, so we could have an hour to watch adult things (I meant Clarkson's Farm. Behave you lot) without worrying that her first word would be something even I would find hard to explain away. A good idea I hear you cry. So why does this suddenly feel like it did not go well?

Gentle reader, knowing Small Child's delight in being contrary, you should have a vague idea where this is going.

7.30pm. I mount the stairs with ill directed confidence. Think Baldrick and a cunning plan, and you will picture the scene well. Small Child is silent. We do the essentials, bottoms and jammies, and settle in for a story. Something gentle about ogres, nothing particularly violent like the Little Mermaid. We aren't making those mistakes again.

7.45pm. There is a noise. It appears to be coming from the general direction of Small Child. It gets louder. Apparently this child has a full and working set of lungs. I suppose we're lucky to have reached this far without knowing this.

8pm. Does this child not need to breathe? I'm fairly sure she has been holding this note for the last fifteen minutes without taking in air. Daddy is lucky he's gone out.

8.15pm. Seriously, where is the volume control? Or failing that, the batteries? Hell, at this point I'll settle for Daddy.

8.30pm. Okay, I take it back. Daddy's helpful suggestion is that I change her nappy. Or feed her. I'm not sure he heard my reply. Or that it would have been particularly helpful for our marriage if he had.

9pm. I've given up. Small Child has now heard the word F*ck more times than she would have if we'd just stayed up. So we might as well watch another episode.

9.45pm. That's it, I've brought out the big guns. I have threatened her with Grandma. Grandma fixes everything. And she is only 5 minutes away. This is the ultimate, end stage threat. I had hoped not to use it until she was at least talking. I may be on the losing side of this war already.

10.30pm. Have I gone deaf? Has the world ended? Had she finally stopped crying? There is nothing as beautiful as silence. Glancing down at her face, I know why.

10.31pm. I have perfected the art of nonchalantly handing over Small Child.

10.32pm. I pretend to be asleep while Daddy makes a discovery that can only be a delivery from Karma after his helpful suggestions at 8.30pm.

10.35pm. Daddy is back. Small Child is asleep, finally. We look at each other. Why do I suspect we will be playing Rock Paper Scissors for the next one?

DAY The Seventeenth (Or Who Mentioned Exercise?)

Gentle reader, we have been at home now for just over two weeks. I have possibly eaten my body weight in all the things I have not been allowed for months. I have even included fruit in this. Not only my own fruit, but other people's too. I even had an orange that previously belonged to some bloke called Terry.

Knowing that I will soon have to appear in public with Small Child, and it is not socially acceptable to do so in pyjamas, I bravely took a step towards fitness. I signed self and Small Child up to a mother and baby exercise class. Apparently one dances while waving one's baby around like a deranged version of Rafiki on speed. In theory, this seems fantastic. In reality, I am as co-ordinated as a three Legged giraffe on ice skates, and Small Child's looks belie her weight.

Thankfully I have until October to find the strength to grapple with Small Child, and also find a sports bra that is up to the task. This may be a herculean task, as I am not sure such a contraption exists. I recall from my youth a company optimistically called Less Bounce. One suspects there was only less bounce if one didn't actually partake in any sport. Turning around too fast could potentially lead to taking some unsuspecting bystander's eye out. As for running, the less said the better.

So there we have it. I must somehow strive to make Bambi on ice look graceful, while preventing a black eye for me, and anyone foolish enough to stand within close range. Pray for me. Pray for those around me. And pass the wine.

DAY The Eighteenth (Or, I Promise She Does Wake Up/It's Possible She Is Faking It)

Gentle reader, it may interest you to know, that Small Child is in possession of some rather beautiful blue eyes. They sparkle, and as her mother, I am well aware that they will be used to her advantage later. At present, they are one of her rather more striking features. People remark on them with regularity. The family in general are of the opinion that they really need to remain blue. My in laws agree.

If only they could see them.

Gentle reader, I hesitate to suggest that my child is being difficult. Or that she has an agenda of her own. However. It has been almost three weeks. They have seen her eyes open once. Twice if we count the fleeting moment she opened them, looked up and immediately shut them again.

She gazes lovingly at our midwife. The health visitor had some rather intense eye contact during her weigh in. My own mother gets the side eye around twice a week when she dares to drink her tea rather than rock Small Child.

She is a past master at opening them the second the in laws leave. Before that? Not a chance. Is it possible she is faking? I'm avoiding asking that question. Is it hilarious? Absolutely.

We currently stand at Small Child 3 In Laws 0. I am almost persuaded that she spent the last 9 months reading The Art of War. Her tactics are impressive, and she shows no mercy. One equally suspects playing "My Way" was a bad idea.

Gentle reader I leave you with this one thought. If she can play us all this well now, Lord help us all when she can talk.

DAY The Nineteenth (Or You Weigh How Much?!)

Gentle reader, today we discovered that Small Child is technically not small. She was a happily average baby upon arrival (albeit one I am glad came out of the sunroof). We were told, with confidence, that she would lose some weight within the first few days. It was at this point we discovered the first inkling of the contrary nature she was harbouring. She decided to do the opposite.

Fast forward to today. She has not only grown into all her larger baby gros, she has added a pound to her weight. This surprised no-one. The amount she is eating, I'm fairly sure she is attempting to outgrow everything she owns in record time. It's either that, or she has worms. Somehow I feel dosing her with panacur would be frowned upon. It has crossed my mind however.

We were informed today, that Small Child shares a birthday with Arnold Schwarzenegger. This is rather apt, as I feel like I need to emulate him to be able to lug her around the house. Baby carrying while preparing breakfast should be an Olympic sport. Buttering bagels with one hand, while bouncing Small Child with the other and fending off any number of opportunistic Beards would surely be a Gold medal winning routine.

I could, perhaps change my breakfast to something more one hand friendly. Gentle reader, I have waited four months for bagels. I will not relinquish them so easily. Baby juggling for the foreseeable it is. Alternatively, I shall buy Grandma Kaegen a saddle.

DAY The Twentieth (Or, We Tried Baby Wearing And It Went As Well As Expected)

Gentle reader, I had an idea. I know. Brace yourselves. Babywearing.

I know it works, I know it will free up my other hand for essential work such as bagel buttering, and I know Small Child will be able to sleep while I do things. What I failed to reckon with is her ability to transform into an octopus at any given moment, and my inability to actually use the damn thing.

It came with instructions. Which of course I read. Or at least I looked at. Firstly they depicted someone who isn't running on a caffeine and chocolate high. This was my first challenge. Secondly they had a baby that was apparently content to be contorted into positions most rhythmic gymnasts would be proud of. And finally, there were no words accompanying said pictures. In other words, it was an IKEA version of a sling.

Picture the scene. A half drunk cup of tea. A baby, throwing shapes that I'm fairly sure it's impossible to get into without a significant amount of alcohol and a whole packet of ibuprofen for the next day, a copious amount of material, and my desire not to swear in front of my child.

Oh, and of course, Zeeva to judge my efforts.

Gentle reader, after what felt like an eternity, we gave up. Small Child shall remain in my arms like a heathen. I could do with the extra weight training after all.

DAY The Twenty First (Or, The One Where Everyone Slept Through Except Mummy)

Gentle reader, we passed an uneventful night. Or at least, Daddy and Small Child did. After a rocky start, where Small Child decided that being awake was infinitely more fun than sleeping in the nursery, Daddy returned triumphant and announced that she was asleep.

Yeah. Right.

After voicing her objections to bedtime, yet again, Mummy waded into battle, clutching a bottle and muttering dire threats which had something to do with Grandma and an orphanage. Daddy was unimpressed when Mummy did actually return triumphant, and Small Child was finally asleep.

Daddy selflessly offered to take the midnight feed. Mummy was delighted.

Midnight came. Daddy slept. So did Small Child. 2am came around, Daddy slept. So did Small Child. 4am passed in the same manner.

A peaceful night! I hear you cry. And yes, for Daddy and Small Child I suspect it was. For Mummy however, who kept getting up to make sure Small Child was still breathing, and to stop herself from smothering Daddy with a pillow, it was less so.

5.30am arrived. Small Child decreed that this was the start of our day. Mummy is OK with this, as Daddy has to now go to football in the rain, and Mummy gets to stay in bed with Small Child and hobnobs.

Mummy may just win after all.

DAY The Twenty Second (Or, The Day Mummy Attempted To Build The Bouncer)

Gentle reader, we decided today that Small Child was old enough to sit in her bouncer. This was hailed as a fantastic idea as it means something other than Mummy can now rock her.

The downside? Mummy had to put it together first. Now, in this household we have very defined roles. Daddy builds things, Mummy supervises. Daddy wields the screwdriver, Mummy drinks the tea. Daddy drops things on his toe, Mummy laughs. You get the idea.

Bravely, Mummy decided to assemble the bouncer under the watchful eye of Daddy, Small Child and Zeeva. Opening the box was the first challenge. Whoever packaged this clearly felt that getting into the box should be equivalent to a Joe Wicks workout.

After triumphantly removing various parts from said box, I sought the instructions with confidence, knowing this would not best me. I had unfortunately not considered the fact that the instructions were vague at best and totally confusing at worst. Equally they were not in English.

Twenty minutes later, and I was waving a metal rod like some form of demented loony. Daddy could not disguise his smirk, as Mummy set down a rather lopsided contraption and proclaimed that it was done.

Daddy laughed. Briefly. With the confidence of Baldrick announcing his next cunning plan, he set about straightening the legs, only to discover that they were not the problem. After grappling with the damn thing for several minutes he reverted to the tried and tested method of bending various bits until it looked vaguely flat, and announced it as a win. He sat back on the sofa in comfort, basking in his glory. After glancing at the box, he seemed surprised to see that it proclaimed that said contraption vibrated. He leapt forward, placed Small Child in and expectantly hit the button. Nothing happened.

His face fell when I told him he had to find batteries first.

DAY The Twenty Second (Or, The One Where Mummy Saw In Every. Single. Hour)

Gentle reader, I fear we were too cocky. We boasted with ill advised confidence of a good night's sleep for Daddy and Small Child. The Gods of Sleep have decreed no more.

Last night Small Child went to bed beautifully at a reasonable hour. There was quiet rejoicing and wine. We even made it into bed ourselves at a normal hour. It was indeed glorious.

In hindsight, we should have realised this did not bode well.

Daddy successfully negotiated the 11.30pm feed in record time. Small Child seemed happy and settled. Again, this should have warned us that troubled waters lay ahead.

At 12.30am Mummy rocked Small Child back to sleep. At 1.20am it was declared that Small Child had not been fed in weeks and was in danger of wasting away. This was dealt with, and Small Child replaced in the cot.
By 2.45am Mummy was out of songs and bedtime stories didn't seem to be cutting it. At 3am, silence reigned and Mummy retreated to bed. This was short lived however, because by 4.15am we were back, on the playmat, just for a change of scene. There were pillows. Cushions. A cup of tea. Muttered threats. Small Child ignored all of them and gurgled happily.

Mummy finally returned to bed at 5.45am, rejoicing in the fact she may get an hour before the aforementioned Small Child decided it was time to start the day. It was not to be. At 6.30am Small Child was up. Again. This time, Daddy braved the onslaught. Mummy, wisely, turned over and went back to sleep. Small Child did not.

It is 10am. We are all awake. Only one of us is happy.

Gentle reader, the moral of this story is simple. When your mother takes great delight in telling you that when you were small, you did not sleep through the night for many years, do not laugh. Just know that Karma has a delivery service. It may take 33 years, but it has a very accurate sat nav.

DAY The Twenty Fourth (Or, Seriously, How Hungry Are You?)

Gentle reader, I fear it will not be long before we cannot call this child Small any longer. My first inkling was when her baby gros did not fit. The second hint came when I tried to pick her up and wondered how I had managed to also pick up a lead weight at the same time. The third and most decisive moment was when the health visitor took one look from across the room and called her a chunky child.

Considering her carefully in the bath this morning I am well aware she can no longer be described as skinny dipping. This Child chunky dunks. She is quite clearly a feminine and more appealing version of the Michelin Man.

I have many, many times been grateful that I am no longer breast feeding. I suspect if I was, I would be heading to the nearest field to stand in sympathy with the neighbourhood cows. As it is, I have a sneaking sympathy with the kettle. It hasn't seen so much use since we started working from home.

Our health visitor, a well meaning and lovely lady, suggested that Small Child should be having around 2 and a half ounce feeds each time, as appropriate to her age. Small Child has very definite objections to this. Namely, that such a small amount is for wimps. Pass the bottle and she'll show you. At this rate she'll be ready to play prop for Wales by the Autumn Internationals (And they could use the help, I'm not gonna lie).

Gentle reader I must fly. I hear ominous gurgles coming from the nursery.

There is no snooze button on a Small Child wanting her second breakfast.

DAY The Twenty Fifth (Or, Zeeva Really Thinks She Could Do Better)

Gentle reader, it has been almost a month that we have been doing this parenting lark. In that time, while I am fully aware that we are winging it, I feel that we have not done badly. Small Child is still living, in fact she is thriving. Proof, in fact, that we might even know what we are doing. Everyone around us has confirmed that this is in fact in the category of a good job.

Then we have Zeeva.

Zeeva, having raised thirteen of her own Puppies, is more than convinced that she can do a better job. From the moment I appear downstairs clutching Small Child, she judges me. I feel her eyes follow me round the room, and if she could speak, I am well aware that she would call me out.

I fell foul of her judgment again today when she realised I planned to allow Small Child to lie in a moses basket without me in close proximity. As if I dared.

I trotted along into the kitchen, preparing to use both hands for a change, when I realised she was blocking my way. She rounded me up, directed me towards the living room and admonished me loudly. When I attempted to return to the kitchen, without Small Child, she assaulted my slippers. When, a third time, I succeeded in making it as far as the sink, she sat in the corner and threw filthy looks my way. Her smug ass look when Small Child made her request for second breakfast known will haunt me for days.

DAY The Twenty Sixth (Or, I Got Her To Bed On Time And Now I Feel Invincible)

Gentle reader today saw a milestone of which I am remarkably proud. For many weeks now, I have been permanently accompanied by some poor soul, tasked with the almost impossible task of making sure I don't overdo things. Tonight however, I was set free. I was left, unaccompanied, unobserved and otherwise wild and free. It was glorious, if a little terrifying.

All I had to do was keep Small Child and Self safe, fed and watered. I even took her for a walk under Hope's watchful eye (although I had the impression she was less than pleased that we returned from the walk still clutching Small Child. If we had lost her along the way, she would not have been overly upset).

The only challenge that remained was to get Small Child to sleep, within vague distance of her proposed bedtime. Friends, you know how this has gone in the past. I was not feeling hopeful.

Gentle reader, the Gods of Bedtime were smiling on me. Not only did Small Child go down on time, but she remained asleep though such events as The Incursion of the Sky Chickens, How Dare Those Leaves Blow In The Front Garden, and Oh Look Daddy Is Home, But Lets Shout At Him Like He Is A Mad Schnauzy Murderer Anyway. She even remained asleep for almost three hours into our bedtime. This is something to be celebrated, as that also included the weekly routine of I Kicked That Damn Box Again, And It Is Only The Fourth Time This Month That I Have Asked You To Move It. It comes with a one footed dance routine, and the language is generally not rated PG.

Now, I am well aware that this feat may never be repeated. This may be the one bedtime that goes down in history, the one we refer to in hushed tones for the rest of our days. I intend to milk it for as long as possible.

Day The Twenty Seventh (Or, Pick Your Battles Wisely)

Gentle reader, last night's antics, unsurprisingly, left me somewhat tired. Small Child and Daddy, equally unsurprisingly, were not.

Bedtime tonight was approached with some trepidation, and the early signs were not good. We put on Jammies, changed bottoms, and had even more to eat.

And we were awake.

Daddy offered to bounce Small Child for a while. This kind offer was declined, for Small Child was not yet deadly quiet. For I am happy to walk miles while Small Child is noisy. Quiet is far more concerning.

Daddy was delighted when Small Child was finally handed into his care. He wondered, briefly, why he was suddenly alone with her.

Mummy knows the signs of impending poo.

Fast forward to this morning. The night feeds, both large in quantity, were carried out by yours truly. Come 7am and Small Child was ready to start the day. Daddy offered to do battle with bottoms while her bath was run.

Gentle reader, it has almost been a month. He has not learnt that when Small Child is handed over with the speed of someone playing pass the parcel, it means danger ahead. Small Child prepared a not inconsiderable surprise for him.

It was a surprise only to him. Friends, it is a good job that the sound of running bathwater masks hysterical laughter.

The moral? Pick your battles wisely friends. For it is better to walk miles and wake through the night than brave the business end of this child. Twice.

DAY The Twenty Eighth (Or, The Day We Surprised A Schnauzer With Hiccups)

Gentle reader, over the past month we have discovered that Small Child is rather fond of hiccups. She indulges in them on regular occasions, and takes great delight in prolonging the event. She has even mastered the art of the sleeping hiccup.

If any of you have ever seen a schnauzer with hiccups, you know it is a fairly hilarious sight. Friends, let me tell you, there is no more hilarity inducing sight than a schnauzer surprised by somebody else's hiccups.

Picture the scene. Small Child, settled and happy on my lap. Schnauzer, equally settled and happy, napping with his head on Small Child. Peace and serenity reigned. Until the hiccups started.

The first was a gentle, trial hiccup. The second came with a little more force. The third was a hiccup of such proportions that it startled said schnauzer spectacularly.

The vertical leap was one of which most Olympic high jumpers would be proud. The look of surprise, a masterpiece. The landing, a solid 8.5.

The dawning realisation, after several minutes of searching for the culprit, that the noise was still emanating from Small Child, was a sight to behold.

Small Child however, to the surprise of nobody around her, remained asleep throughout.

Gentle reader, I long for a day without a hiccup marathon. But today, today made up for it.

DAY The Twenty Ninth (Or, The Day I Argued With Alexa About Rain Sounds)

Gentle reader, a useful tool for settling Small Child at night has been Alexa. She has a wide range of uses, from turning the light on, to bringing the crooning tones of Mr Sinatra into the room, to reminding me that it's a ridiculous time in the morning and I am still awake.

This week however, we discovered something that is a game changer. Rain sounds.

I know what you are thinking. We live in Wales. Rain sounds have been the soundtrack to our lives for the last thirty years at least. The Bible talks about it raining for forty days and forty nights, and that's still the driest summer on record.

I digress.

For three nights, Alexa had been a team player, obliging with said sounds at the merest suggestion. Until last night. Last night, I requested that she provide, and instead of her usual response, she immediately leapt into a spiel about rain. While she had interesting facts that I had never known, 3am is not the best time to be presenting them. Three times we did this dance, during which, Small Child became so bored with our conversation that she fell asleep.

This should have been the end of it. After all, the goal of sleeping baby had been achieved. Gentle reader, it is well known that I do not know when I'm beaten.

Equally it seems, I do not know when I have won. I was determined to have the last word. A final request for rain sounds followed. I suspect the threat to disconnect at the plug via scissors, muttered under my breath in round three, had been taken on board. I retired to bed happy, until Small Child decided she was hungry.

DAY The Thirtieth (Or, She Is The Reason My Tea Was Cold For The First Time)

Gentle reader, today we attended Small Child's first social function, the Village Tea Party. When I say we, what I really mean is that Daddy and I were there purely as her support act. Barely had we sat ourselves at a convenient table, when a rush ensued. The line that had formerly been for the buffet became a baby visiting queue. Many times I looked longingly at my cup of tea, which was quietly reaching lukewarm, but knew it was a futile exercise trying to drink it.

Gentle reader, I had no idea that baby slings would be a topic on which I would become an expert; however I now know what my specialist subject would be on Mastermind.

Many times we described how blue Small Child's eyes are, while people peeked at her cherubic little face. Did she have the common decency to wake up and bestow a glance on her admirers?

Did she hell. Her first social outing and even asleep she was still more of a hit than the rest of us. Is this a glimpse into the future? Am I to spend eternity as a backup act to my own daughter? Will she forever garner such attention from all she meets? Has she the skills to captivate any and all people in a specified area? I have no qualms with this. Daddy on the other hand, is now pre-emptively researching shotguns.

DAY The Thirty First (Or, I Put My Baby In A Grow Bag)

Gentle reader, we have now been in sole charge of this Small Child for a month. One could describe it as a learning curve, if we accept that it's the sort of curve that one finds at the top of a rather nasty surprise drop on a roller-coaster. However, we have made it this far. All three of us are still intact, and the only one with a predilection for the bottle appears to be the youngest. We'll we start as we mean to go on in this family.

This evening, we had a bright idea. Knowing that Small Child has been putting away a significant amount of the good stuff over the last few days, and therefore could confidently be described as having a growth spurt, we decided that our best move would be to insert her into a grow bag overnight.

We have long joked about these things in our family, as the gene pool in the latter generation on one side has long been short changed (pun intended) in the matter of height. The other side of the family have not been described as tall since they left The Shire.

And so it was decided, to give Small Child a fighting chance of ever reaching the top shelf without a stepladder, that a grow bag would be employed. I stopped short of adding compost and putting her in the green house for one reason alone.

We don't have a greenhouse.

DAY The Thirty Second (Or, Naked Baby, Round Three)

Gentle reader, today we played yet another round of Naked Baby Roulette. I went into it with not ill placed confidence, as the last we left the last round honours even.

Small Child however, was keen to redress the balance.

Having prepared a bath of the appropriate depth and temperature (for those curious, Small Child likes it deep and warm), I prepared to to battle. My first job was to remove clothes from said Child, and deal with any surprises she felt necessary to present me with. The fact she gave me nothing should, in hindsight, have been my first warning.

Clutching Small Child, I began the dangerous walk to the bathroom, Naked Baby firmly ensconced in my arms. We paused to wave at Daddy and wiggle a Naked Baby at him. This brought about my second warning. Small Child fired a warning shot, which I will be forever thankful is best described as all sound and fury. I have never cleared the remaining 5 metres to the bath so quickly.

Gentle reader, you will be pleased to hear we made it without any notable incident. Round Three seemed to be chalked up as a win.

Having plonked Small Child on her bare behind in the bath, I rejoiced. Too soon Gentle reader, too soon. Round Four shall forever be known as The Water Round. At the time of writing, it is Mummy 2 Small Child 3.

The war continues.

DAY The Thirty Third (Or, The One Where We All Had Five Hours Sleep)

Gentle reader; remember when Daddy and Small Child had a beautiful night's sleep? The night that frankly, everyone except me slept through for a good four hours? We have not only replicated it, but surpassed it.

Small Child had a busy day. She spent the morning charming the village at the monthly coffee morning (yes, there was more cake. No, my post baby diet isn't going well), and spent the afternoon strolling the canal with Huzzah, delighting passers by. Her social diary is quite full these days, and obviously being the centre of attention is draining.

She also declined to nap for more than half an hour at a time, leaving those of us charged with her care fearing the worst come bedtime.

By those of us, I of course mean me. Daddy swanned off to five aside, leaving Self and Small Child alone for this particular battle.

Bottoms came and went, jammies were on. Bedtime stories were read, and when all else failed, Uncle Frank was called upon. When Daddy returned, we had napped for half an hour, and were now tucking into what turned out to be the equivalent to a five course meal.

And then she passed out.

Five hours later, and I was confused. How was it 3am? When last I looked, it was 10pm. That I was sure of. A quick return of the bottle, and by quick I mean 5oz later, and we were all back in bed.

Who is this, and what have they done with Small Child?

Daddy asked why I was rejoicing so gladly, if a little confusedly. He questioned if this was any different to normal, as he is sure he doesn't wake between the midnight feed and breakfast, and nearly started the day being smothered by a convenient pillow.

DAY The Thirty Fourth (Or, When Will I Learn Not To Boast About Sleeping?)

Gentle reader, you know what I am about to relate. In hindsight, we all knew exactly what was going to happen after I reported the five hour sleep with such joy.

Clearly Small Child enjoyed her sleep so very much, that the best thing she could do was to continue sleeping for the majority of the day as well. Staying awake simply was not on her agenda. This was not for lack of trying on my part however.

Old Macdonald, sung loudly, tunelessly, with the appropriate noises, did nothing to stop her eyes from closing. A vigorous round of Row Row Row Your Boat, Zoom Zoom Zoom and Incy Wincy Spider, with actions, produced no useful response.

Abandoning Small Child in the moses basket and putting the kettle on, usually a recipe for her realizing it is time to produce the world's biggest wee, and therefore requiring everyone in the vicinity to know about it, failed to elicit a single solitary reaction.

Gentle reader, by 11am I knew we were screwed. By 2pm, when Small Child had been awake for but a handful of hours (and not all in one go), I warned Daddy of the possibility of a long night. At 6pm, he ducked out and went to football, promising to do all feeds and wake ups prior to midnight.

A generous offer you cry. Gentle reader, allow me to fill you in on Small Child's bedtime routine. A Bath at 6.30. Jammies and a story before 7. By 8, I have usually persuaded her to pass out. 11pm she realises she is starved and unloved, and requires immediate attention.

Do you see where this is leading oh Gentle reader? Daddy selflessly offering to do all before midnight is one thing. There are just a lot more hours between midnight and 7.30am.

I have not yet understood why he is not available post midnight. Unless he fears our Small Child is a gremlin, and wishes no part in the potential mayhem.

He wouldn't be far wrong.

DAY The Thirty Fifth (Or, Surely The Whole Point Of Dream Feeding Is That You Stay Asleep?)

Gentle reader, in an attempt to cut down on the amount to time we are collectively awake at night; we have begun to embrace the dream feed. This requires only one of us to have our eyes open at any one time.

Or at least, that's the vague idea.

It has been five weeks. You know Small Child's personality well by now. Obviously she didn't get the whole memo, or if she did, it wasn't a message she wanted to take on board.

She has mastered the art of feeding and winding while acting like she is 90% asleep. She does this well enough for me to be convinced each and every time, that this time we've cracked it. We even have a little safety rock for five minutes, just to be sure. I approach the cot, place her in it, and take a step back, preparatory to making a swift exit in the direction of sleep.

Gentle reader, when will I learn? Never, never look back. Because I know full well that Small Child will be wide awake, staring right back at me.

So far, the only one to have successfully kept their eyes shut throughout each and every dream feed has been Daddy.

I'm more than slightly jealous.

DAY The Thirty Sixth (Or, Have You Ever Wrestled A Dead Weight Octopus Into A Bag?)

Gentle reader, if you fancy a challenge of epic proportions, go to your local beach, find a convenient octopus, and a bag, and proceed to insert said octopus into it.

Oh how easy I hear you cry. I can do this with my eyes closed.

I'm pleased to hear that, as the other half of this challenge is to do it at 3am, after staying awake for a month, with nothing but an ikea night light to help you. Just for added excitement, the bag keeps shrinking with each attempt.

Oh, and the octopus is on an LSD trip, and waving various tentacles appropriately.

Gentle reader, you now have an accurate picture of how it feels to change Small Child's nappy at 3am.

This Child has the uncanny ability to be both dead weight, and LSD octopus in the leg department at any one time. It would be impressive, if I wasn't attempting to insert said legs into a baby gro and then a sleep bag. The added talent of grabbing anything within reach and holding into it for grim death while waving her arms about was amusing to start with. After being whacked with a spare nappy twice, the amusement grew old, fast.

Let's just take a moment and be thankful it was a spare nappy.

DAY The Thirty Seventh (Or, The Day I Walked 5000 Steps On The Landing)

Gentle reader, as you know, we have been the envy of our friends lately, as the Gods of Sleep have seen fit to bestow on us a child who actually sleeps for prolonged periods. We have been grateful, oh so grateful. We also knew that this blessing was probably fleeting. After a week of 5 hour naps overnight, we knew there was trouble ahead.

Equally, those of you who have been paying close attention to these missives, you may remember that I have signed Self and Small Child up to an exercise class.

As an aside, we are no closer to solving the sports bra dilemma, at this rate duct tape is starting to look appealing. Anyhow, I digress.

Small Child and the Gods of Sleep have finally seen fit to bestow what one can only call, in comparison to our usual, a long ass night. It appears that part of our punishment is to start exercising earlier than planned.

Small Child has decided that sleep is for the weak. Her requirements for a good night apparently include the slowest marathon known to man. I have paced up and down the landing until I have worn tracks in the carpet. Foolishly I looked at my step counter.

While sleep is for the weak, walking 5k steps in your slippers is a skill.

DAY The Thirty Eighth (Or, So We Were Forced To Up The Stakes In The Naked Baby Game)

Gentle reader, as those of you with school age children know, summer has returned. This is evident, not by the fact Facebook is flooded by first day pictures, but because the sun is shining. And not only shining, it's bloody boiling.

Normally, I would be basking at this point, however Small Child is, as yet, too young to emulate a lizard, or Zeeva, and must stay in the cool. This is not a huge problem, as it is a ready made excuse to binge watch Death In Paradise.

Now, as the temperature climbed today, Small Child became uncomfortable. Indoors was not enough. It was time to play Naked Baby.

Gentle reader, we have a cream carpet downstairs, to match the same carpet upstairs, which as you know has become the Naked Baby Gauntlet pre bath time. While a short dash from one end of the landing to another is one thing, actively having Naked Baby over a carpet for prolonged periods is a very dangerous move.

We bounced. We sang. We wiggled. Naked Baby was naked. Daddy looked in, and hurriedly left. He wanted no part in this madness.

I am delighted to announce that Mummy won this round, and the carpet remains unscathed. We pray for cooler weather, for the odds will not always be in our favour.

DAY The Thirty Ninth (Or, The Day Mummy Returned To Exercise And Nearly Died)

Gentle reader, today saw me attempt to return to some sort of normality post Small Child. Prior to her arrival I had been a fixture in my local pool, twice a week, waving my arms and legs about in a fashion reminiscent of a daddy long legs partially stuck in glue. This was not me attempting to swim (I'm actually half decent at that), oh no, this was aqua aerobics. A contingent of 25 ladies, singing and wiggling, sometimes with weights, sometimes with woggles. It was a sight to be seen. And never forgotten.

This continued until around two weeks before Small Child made her grand entrance. As I became more heavily pregnant, there was less wiggling and more existing, whale like, while others, including my midwife and my mother, wiggled around me. It would have continued right up until the arrival of Small Child, however there was a costume fitting incident. One week it fitted beautifully, the following week I appeared to require a costume the size of Belgium. But anyway.

Bravely (Or foolishly, the line is a fine one, and I frequently use it as a skipping rope) I decided the time was ripe for a return to the water. Gracefully, like the proverbial walrus, I entered, and prepared to wiggle.

Gentle reader, I had forgotten one thing. Due to the nature of Small Child's arrival, I have no stomach muscles. None. Zero. Nada. 45 minutes later and I was even more acutely aware of this fact. Who knew you needed them to move your legs? And as for getting back out of the pool, forget it. I managed that with the grace of a manatee doing a forward roll on land.

I would like to say I enjoyed it. I would be lying. Worryingly, I have agreed to return next week. Am I mad?

On second thoughts, don't answer that question.

DAY The Fortieth (Or, What Is This Bedtime Of Which You Speak? I Know It Not)

Gentle reader, as you may, or may not, be aware, we share this house with a not insignificant number of dogs. A sane person has one. Those who like being pulled in different directions around a lamppost, have two. Occasionally, some have taken leave of their senses long enough to think three is a good idea. Me personally, I have five of the bearded financial burdens, plus a part time indoor bear. I'm a special kind of crazy.

Why is this relevant to Small Child? Routine. That's why.

One cannot survive living with these canine pirates, who mutiny and demand food with menaces, without some semblance of a routine. They may run wild from dawn till dusk, but come 9pm, they are in bed. We even get dirty looks for trying to stay up late. This we felt, would translate well to Small Child.

Brimming with confidence and hope, we put together a bedtime routine. There's a bath. A story. Jammies. Milk. On a Friday, there's even gin. To our eternal delight, it usually works. Some time between 7.30 and 8pm, Small Child passes out. It's happened often enough for us to claim it is not a fluke.

That brings us to tonight. Tonight Small Child has decided to throw bedtime in the bin. Why, why would one want to go to sleep, when one could stay up and watch Killer in My Village with mummy? Surely it's more fun to make mummy pace the floor repeatedly, fake falling asleep at the critical moment, and wake up the second you are placed in your cot, ensuring mummy never finds out who did it.

Gentle reader, we may have been blessed with a child that sleeps, and for this reason be the envy of all our friends, it's just that getting her there takes fourteen different positions, prayers to all the gods and a sacrificial goat.

Tonight, I need a bigger goat.

DAY The Forty Something Or Other (Or, Dream Feeds Are Good For My Waistline)

Gentle reader, last night was yet another milestone in the world of Small Child. Not just a five hour sleep, but two, yes two, dream feeds.

In other words, I almost got as much sleep as Daddy.

Gentle reader, dream feeding is a game changer. Not only does it mean we are up and down faster than a schnauzer running away from a bath, but it means there is less late night hobnob consumption going on. Normally I would denounce this as madness, as sneaky hobnob consumption is one of my special skills. However, in under three weeks I have to appear in public in a skirt suit. Preferably one that does up. As it stands, I have many, many suits. They fit their hangers perfectly.

I, unfortunately, am not a hanger. Things must change, and sharpish. The hobnobs and I shall continue to share a room, but will practice social distancing at all times. If I can manage to eat a hobnob from six feet away and without touching it, it will be such a feat of magnificence that it shall be allowed. At that point, I'll have two.

As I sit here, with a dozing Small Child, I have realised the unintended consequences of dream feeds. We have not changed a nappy yet.

Between the face on Small Child and the noises emanating from the other end, I suspect I will regret being the one awake.

DAY The Forty Third I Think (Or, How To Bring Up Your Child Properly).

Gentle reader, since birth we have decided to instil in Small Child two very important things. Firstly, a love of reading. We thought that starting her off with fairy stories was a good idea. You all know how that went down. I'm still traumatised.

The second thing we have decided is of great importance, is an eclectic taste in music. She is already a fan of the crooners. Uncle Frank has seen us through many a nappy change. Mr Armstrong accompanies us to the bathroom, his soothing tones often at odds with the speed at which we cross the landing. I have also, in deference to the much-reduced age of the listening audience, made my Spotify play list rather more PG. Remembering to sing the baby friendly words however is more of a challenge.

Anyhow.

Today I decided the time was ripe for advancing Small Child's musical education, and inadvertently Daddy's. Having exhausted the likes of Baa Baa Black Sheep, I Am The Music Man and various other musical greats, and moved swiftly through Frank Sinatra, Daddy returned home from the morning dog walk to hear Birdhouse In Your Soul. This one he knows. Captain Beaky took him by surprise. His expression when we moved on to Star Trekkin had to be seen to be believed. I don't know what distressed him more. That Alexa would play them, that I knew all the words, or that I seem hell bent on teaching them to Small Child.

I have yet to expose him to My Dingaling.

DAY The Forty Fourth (Or, Is That Noise The Floorboards Or My Knees?)

Gentle reader, it may have come to your attention that I am not as young as I used to be. Despite not adding last year to my age as I did not use it, I appear to me rushing wantonly into my mid-thirties. Lately I have become more aware of this onrushing of the years through one simple fact. Everything aches.

This brings us to last night. Last night was not a night for pacing with Small Child. She was quite content to remain in the nursery, and be rocked. This, I concurred, was an excellent idea. So we began.

Left, right, creak. Left, right, crunch. Left, right, creak.

I stopped, much to Small Child's displeasure. We took a step or two to the left.

Left, right, creak. Left, right, crunch.

Now, I am aware we live in an old house. The floorboards in Small Child's nursery are older than I am. I am aware that at times, usually when one is trying to creep about quietly to eat hobnobs, they groan like a medieval Knight being sat on by a donkey of solid proportions. I assumed that self, plus Small Child, were simply applying pressure to said warped boards.

Imagine my consternation when, on placing Small Child down to sleep, and avoiding stepping on anything remotely creaky, this noise followed me.

Gentle reader, while our floorboards are old, it seems my knees are convinced they are equally decrepit and are currently challenging them to a creak-off. That would be fine, except I have 10lb of Small Child over one shoulder. Will she accept the rocking chair as a substitute? Will she hell. Will she accept a style of rocking that does not involve the transference of our combined weight onto on leg? You know she won't.

Small Child is an equal opportunities employer. She is giving me ample opportunity to make sure both shoulders ache, and both knees creak with equal force. I feel I cannot ask for any sort of concessions. This would be seen as a sign of weakness.

DAY The Forty Fifth (Or, How Can You Fall Asleep That Fast When It Suits You?)

Gentle reader, Small Child has long been lauded as looking just like her Daddy. Her attitude however, is often described as all my own. This is an unfortunate combination when you consider Daddy's hairline and how exhausted my parents look.

Now, as a rule, Small Child has been a delight when it comes to bedtime and all things sleep related. Last night was what one could describe as middling. We may have only demanded feeding twice, but we made those feeds count. Not only did Small Child put away a significant amount each time, she decided to stay awake to enjoy both them and the night time ambience. Convincing her to go back to sleep saw me singing songs from the Lion King (somewhat inspired by her sleeping bag I will admit), and rocking more than a ferry on the Irish Sea.

This brings me to this morning. Small Child, knowing Daddy had to leave early today, decided that six thirty was the best time to go back to sleep. And down she went like a stone. Fast forward to 8.30 and she stirs. Hearing this, and seeing her eyes open when I check on her, I think, I know, I'll get her bath ready for her.

The bath is drawn. The bubbles are ready.

She is asleep. Again.

Gentle reader, how can it take four and a half days, fifteen changes in position and a sacrificial goat to get this child to sleep in the middle of the night, yet when she feels the need, she can drop off in the space of a bath being run?! There is only one other person I know who can achieve this feat.

Seems she takes after Daddy in more than just looks.

DAY The Forty Sixth (Or, I Need To Step Away From My Debit Card)

Gentle reader, I have a confession to make. It is entirely possible that I am spoiling Small Child. It's either that, or I have an unhealthy relationship with Mr Amazon.

I have always been partial to a bit on online shopping, that is no great secret. Prior to the arrival of Small Child, I had a slight collar obsession. My greatest fear in life was that if I died, my husband would sell my collar collection for what I told him I had paid for them. Now however, I have discovered that buying clothes suitable for Small Child is far more fun.

We have already reached the point where she requires an extra room for her clothes, but this has not yet deterred me. The options for pretty little girl clothes appear endless, and I have no will power. It would not be so bad if her outfits only came in one colour. And we haven't even started on toys yet.

I assumed that simply putting my card out of reach would be enough, as I am essentially a lazy soul, and walking into another room would be too much effort. This would have been fine, until my phone helpfully started remembering my card number.

Gentle reader, I know my delivery drivers by name. This is not good. I don't need six months away from work. I need six months away from my debit card. That's what I really need.

Because by then she'll need a whole new wardrobe...

DAY The Forty Seventh (Or, Forget Solar, Wind Power Is Where It's At)

Gentle reader, an indelicate matter is the subject of today's missive. While Small Child is, of course, a delight in all ways, it has come to my attention that during our nightly feeds, she is capable of providing enough wind to power at least half of Powys.

If we had kept it to the top end of Small Child, that would have been preferable. This was not to be. Twice this night alone we have almost achieved lift off. NASA would be proud. We have even altered our post feed positioning, as this was not something I needed in my ear.

It was with some trepidation that, at 4am, I approached the business end of Small Child. After all, these gastric gymnastics could not come without a price, and a fairly hefty one at that.

To my everlasting delight, it appears that Small Child has fully embraced the ethos of it being all sound and fury, signifying nothing.

I'm still making Daddy do the morning change though. Just in case.

DAY The Forty Eighth (Or, Why Is There Always A Spider At 3am?)

Gentle reader, as you know, this house is not solely populated by humans. We share this happy space with five and a half four legged financial burdens. We co-exist peacefully, and nobody tries to steal the custard creams. It's a good system. What I haven't mentioned, is that we also seem to have acquired a spider.

Now, I am not a fearful soul. I love this Small Child dearly. I would take a bullet for her, jump in front of a train, even sell my husband if needs be, but when it comes to spiders, she's on her todd. It's every man for himself, as Daddy has learnt over the past 8 years.

At 3am precisely, the beast makes an entrance. I don't know if it thinks we have a standing date, or that this is just the family meeting time. It might be a concerned parent, come to offer advice and support. It is entirely possible that it is a sociable creature, and merely wants to debate local politics. I wouldn't know, I haven't stopped to ask, and I do not intend to.

This nightly visit is the main reason Small Child has learnt to self soothe. It appears, I leave. If Small Child happens to be asleep at the time, that's a bonus. If not, then that's on her. You may find this an extreme reaction oh Gentle reader, however you haven't seen the spider.

If it was any bigger, I'd make up the back bedroom and be charging it rent.

DAY The Forty Ninth (Or, Please Don't Nap Right Before Bedtime)

Gentle reader, as you know, Small Child and I have found a rather good routine. Right down to our co-parenting spider visit. We have perfected this over the last few weeks, and have been feeling rather smug. Small Child feeds and naps on schedule, and is all singing and dancing when Daddy gets home. Her last nap is 4pm, and this is purely to charge the batteries before Daddy's arrival at 5.15.

Until today. Today, naps have been for the weak. Today we decided that half an hour here or there would absolutely do. Apparently her batteries only required fast charging today. Mummy's may have required more, but that does not figure in Small Child's daily plan.

As the evening drew in, and bedtime grew ever closer, I began to feel optimistic. Surely the dearth of daytime naps would play out in our favour. Knowing Small Child as I do, I did not dare mention this out loud for fear of her hearing it and deciding that this was not what she had signed up for.

Daddy on the other hand....

Gentle reader, it was forty minutes before bedtime. Of course that was the perfect time to pass out. Why not. Clearly I will have words with this Small Child when she regains consciousness. I will also have words with Daddy about stating the obvious within Small Child's hearing. Until then, pass the wine. We're clearly going nowhere.

DAY The Fiftieth (Or Thank The Lord For Laminate Flooring)

Gentle reader; cast your mind back to one or two of our earliest missives. I recounted the story of Daddy VomitGate, and my hilarity upon reaching the top of the stairs. The second which I require you to call to mind, is the one where we discovered how accurate Karma's delivery service was.

You know where I am headed with this.

Having decided she was hungry, Small Child demanded her bottle in an insistent manner. I obliged, and saw 3oz disappear within the sort of time frame Usain Bolt would be proud of. Following this, we wandered into the kitchen to see how Daddy was getting on with tea. In hindsight, this was a strong move.

An ominous rumble. A Hiccup. Gentle reader, I knew. Let's just say I had the foresight to have her over my shoulder. Gatland came within an inch of needing a bath. Daddy could only watch in horror, muttering something about having only steam mopped the floor twenty four hours earlier.

With a hip movement that even Craig Revel Horwood couldn't criticise, I avoided being covered. The freezer was not so lucky.

Gentle reader, it was spectacular. I neatly avoided having to clean up, and made my getaway, with Small Child in tow, leaving Daddy to wield the kitchen roll in a manner reminiscent of medieval knights.

The look on Small Child's face when we swapped out milk for water to settle her down again, let's just say, it's a good job she can't talk yet.

DAY The Fifty First (Or, Taking A Handprint Is Harder Than You Think)

Gentle reader, as many of you may have noticed, Small Child is growing at an alarming rate. Not only are we galloping headlong into the eight week mark, but we are about to outgrow yet another set of baby gros.

Now, like many doting parents before us, we decided that we would mark the occasion by taking imprints of Small Child's hands and feet. We have baby safe ink pads, card, and there are two of us and one of her.

What could possibly go wrong?

Sensibly, we took the foot print first. It was quite simple. Expose foot. Grab foot. Shove foot on pad. Remove foot (from pad, not from Small Child), plonk on card. Voilà.

And so to the hand print.

We approached this with ill placed confidence. We had already successfully navigated the kicking end after all. We used similar tactics, with one of us brandishing the ink pad, the other preparing to place said appendage on it. Gentle reader, what we failed to realise is that Small Child had other ideas. We were not aware that this was about to turn into a wrestling match with something akin to a dead weight octopus. While I am well practiced with inserting a dead weight octopus into a bag (as you may remember from our earlier communications), this time there was ink.

Small Child's hands may be small, but dear lord can she spread ink everywhere, and in a very short time. The clenched fist ensured that every part of her hand, front and back had an even covering. Rubbing her face saw an interesting pattern develop. And grabbing her clothing firmly ensured the washing machine got a look in. Reaching out to hold onto any part of mummy she could find, just convinced me that she was sharing the love.

Gentle reader, I have often been asked how I get five dogs to sit and look at a camera in perfect unison. The answer? Witchcraft and bribery. If I can manage this not inconsiderable feat, how is it impossible to take a simple hand print from a recumbent child? I suspect I will have to sneak up on her while she dozes. Given that this child feels that daytime naps are for the weak, this could be interesting.

DAY The Fifty-Somethingth (Or, I Have Raised The Bar For Tiredness)

Gentle reader, being a newborn parent is tiring. The 10lb dungaree wearing dictator is a delight, but she feels naps are not an essential part of our daily routine. I feel that they are. This is not the only thing we disagree on when it comes to sleep, but I digress.

Today, I felt like I had this parenting lark nailed. I not only got out of the house on time, I made it to the GP surgery early. Small Child was impeccably behaved during the appointment, and I felt that life was good. Riding this cloud of achievement, I headed to Aldi, knowing I would be able to achieve the impossible. I would get only what was on my shopping list, and not a paint your own garden gnome, a trumpet or a hedge trimmer. I would, in fact, miss out the middle aisle all together.

Gentle reader, I did exactly that. For the second time in my life, I did not succumb to the myriad of delights that I never knew I needed. Flush with triumph, I headed for the car.

Carefully, I unloaded the bottom of the pram, so as not to wake the sleeping Small Child. I stowed her safely into her car seat, made sure the pram was securely in, and retrieved the Aldi leaflet from the floor where I dropped it. Driving home, I planned my afternoon, taking full advantage of my functioning adulthood, starting with putting the shopping away before walking a dog or two. Leaping from my car, I threw open the sliding door to expose... The lack of shopping.

Gentle reader, I am currently operating at a level of tired that shall henceforth be known as Tired Enough To Leave Your Shopping In The Car Park In Aldi.

DAY The Fifty-Somethingth (Or, The One Where Daddy Does The Work, But Mummy Gets The Glory)

Gentle reader, sleep is a coveted thing in this house. While Small Child does this well once convinced it is in her best interests, you already know of our challenges to get her into this state. Stories and songs are not enough for this child. Bath time is simply wet playtime. Soporific, it ain't.

This brings us to last night. Last night it was Daddy's turn for jammies and bedtime while I was woggle wiggling in the water. Upon arriving home, some forty minutes past the assigned Jammies time, I discover Daddy locked in a battle of wills with Small Child, and not on the winning side.

Small Child was indeed in Jammies, and was also ensconced in her grow bag. She was also giving full voice to her opinions about this development. What she and Daddy appeared to be disagreeing about, was both a bottle, and the plan to sleep following it.

Handing off Small Child, Daddy was clearly unimpressed with my claim that she was hungry, having been waving a bottle at her for the last half an hour at least. Imagine, if you will, his face, when Small Child inhaled a rather large amount of milk, burped loudly, and passed out.

Six hours later, she requested a top up, and another nap. A popular Small Child with Daddy she was not. I on the other hand, found it hilarious.

If only we'd had that six hour sleep before I went to Aldi.

DAY The Fifty-Somethingth Else (Or, That Hot Tub Has Been Calling Me)

Gentle reader, I am in the fortunate position of having a hot tub. A proper all singing, all dancing, hard sided hot tub. By that I mean my neighbour has it, and as she and I are basically the same person, it's also mine. Prior to Small Child making her existence known back in November of last year, it's safe to say that said neighbour and I lived in said tub. There may have been a resident bottle of gin or two to complete the party.

It has been ten months since I last sank into it's depths, thanks in no small part to Small Child, so tonight I gaily handed bedtime off to Daddy and gadded off next door.

I managed to avoid any mention of bottoms, jammies or sleep. I threw parenting responsibilities and cares to the wind and left Daddy to it. Knowing how well the previous attempts had been, I was not expecting any great success in this department.

Gentle reader, I was wrong. Daddy, wiser in his day and generation, had learnt from his latest defeat. His tactics were those of a pro, and Small Child could not resist. Sleep was over coming her and she was not fighting it. What had changed so spectacularly in the past 24 hours? Daddy's master stroke? Wearing Mummy's dressing gown.

A butterfly covered indigo dressing gown and boot slippers is quite a look. And not one I was expecting.

I quite like it.

DAY The Fifty-Somethingth Again (Or, Into The Cot Awake Shall Ye Go. And Ye Shall Like It)

Gentle reader, as you are aware, Small Child has long mastered the art of dream feeding. Frankly I am jealous. To not even have to wake up for food, yet knowing it will be provided on schedule? Surely this is in fact, the dream.

Small Child has had become so adept at this, that even I only have to keep one eye open while the event is happening. It is glorious.

However.

Lately Small Child has discovered that she can play us like the proverbial fiddle. She feeds and burps with her eyes tight shut. The five minute safety rock to ensure she is down is accepted in the same manner. And then comes the put down. Just as you tuck the blanket around her for that extra toasty feeling... Bing. Eyes wide open.

Gentle reader, at 2am, it's a good job she is cute. Now, I know what you're thinking. Where is this tough love, of the style I am known to give my dogs, and occasionally, mostly after football, my husband? Digging into the attitude that I have in abundance, this very night, I played Small Child at her own game. Small Child was placed, with all due ceremony, into her cot. The blanket was appropriately tucked. The eyes, oh the eyes opened. As they did, the lights went off and gaily I trotted bed wards, leaving Small Child to ponder her life choices.

Of course, she is probably already asleep, while I sit and pen this missive, so I have gained exactly nothing in terms of additional sleep. I'm trying not to think about that.

DAY The Fifty-Somethingth Once More (Or, Eight Weeks In And Still Functioning)

Gentle reader, it has been eight weeks since Small Child made her arrival into our lives. I remember what sleep was like, I think. I used to like it. I vaguely remember having shoulders that were level and a neck that didn't tip sideways.

Being held under the sway of a 10lb dictator in a Lion King sleep bag is a learning curve, if said curve was at the top of a blind drop on a roller coaster, when you're not wearing a seat belt and the track under consideration is of questionable age and repair.

Today I attempted to groom a hound or two, while Small Child supervised. She judged my efforts in a way not dissimilar to Zeeva's scrutiny of my parenting skills, and I am not sure she approved. I have yet to tell her that she is joining us at an ungodly hour of the morning tomorrow and will be making her debut into the show world.

Knowing how contrary Small Child delights in being, and considering I have to wake her up at 4.30am, I fully expect tonight to be the night she plans to sleep through.

Pray for my soul.

DAY The Fifty-Somethingth Again (Or, Welcome To How We Spend Our Weekends Kid)

Gentle reader, as you might have been aware, we have several four legged financial burdens. Living with these bearded wonders is somewhat like living on a pirate ship. There is a fair bit of drinking, swearing, and regular mutiny from the little raiders I've created. Safe to say, Small Child fits in perfectly. Her personal favourite is Brother Gatties, who unfortunately I have to take sole credit for as his breeder. While Zeeva feels secure enough to judge my parenting skills, I have to remind her on a daily basis that he is actually her son. She has yet to respond in a maternal manner, and frankly I can't blame her.

Anyhow.

Much to the confusion of Daddy when we first met, my main hobby, other than gin, is paying extortionate amounts of money for the privilege of running in an anticlockwise direction in a field, clutching a dog in one hand, and with fridge raiders in my bra, whilst wearing a suit. In other words, I show dogs.

Gentle reader, I felt that the time was ripe to introduce Small Child to this world. After all, I now have four dogs to show. I'm going to need a handler, and she really ought to start earning her keep. And how bad could it be? I mean, 4.30am is a perfectly normal time to be up and on the road.

Small Child was appropriately dressed in a Best In Show baby gro, and a vest depicting Brother Gatties. One has to aim high. While she may not have been thrilled at the prospect of spending all day in a barn, she only gave me side eye twice.

Prior to introducing Small Child to this world of hairspray and madness, we had set her up a pension and a trust fund. Why is this relevant you ask?

Well, the only way to become a millionaire while showing dogs, is to start out a billionaire.

DAY The Fifty Ninth (Or, I Argued With Alexa Over Nothing)

Gentle reader, you recall perhaps that as part of our parenting strategy, we have enlisted the help of Alexa. She has many uses, from crooning along during nappy changes, to reminding you it's a ridiculous hour of the morning, and turning the dining room lights on and off from the nursery, when you accidentally mention the wrong room at 3am.

You may also recall that she and I had a rather heated exchange regarding rain sounds. That round was an unequivocal win for me. Since then, Alexa has been keeping a low profile. Rain sounds have been provided without additional preamble for some weeks now.

Gentle reader, it pains me to tell you that after last night, we stand firmly at one all. I have lost the moral high ground.

Small Child was sleeping, and had been for some time. With this I was delighted, and so felt that she no longer required rain sounds. I instructed Alexa in a whisper to turn them off. She did not comply. I repeated my request, in a similar manner. Again, she ignored me. Raising my voice somewhat, I uttered the same phrase. Nada. Inserting an expletive, I indicated what Alexa could do with her rain sounds if she did not acquiesce with my request for them to be turned off. Somewhat stubbornly, she continued to act as if I was not there.

I left the room, thinking things that would be unprintable on radio, with the intent of summoning Daddy to fix the unrepentant technology. Halfway down the stairs I stopped. Why, why could I still hear rain sounds so clearly? What was this witchcraft? Gazing out of the hall window I realised something.

It was actually raining.

DAY The Sixtieth (Or, You Don't Half Pick Your Moments Child)

Gentle reader, as we have previously discovered, Small Child has impeccable timing. VomitGate One and it's sequel, VomitGate: Revenge Of The Baby, have shown this to be true. Usually I celebrate these occasions, enjoying the fact that this child has comedic timing that Dawn French would be proud of.

This leads us to today.

Gentle reader, it may surprise you to learn that I do not spend my entire day pandering to Small Child. Other things demand my attention, and they all have beards and loud voices.

I deemed the time was ripe to place the largest of these into the bathtub and assault it with shampoo. And when I say "place", I mean beg that she gets in unassisted, because I am NOT lifting 36kg of attitude. I made the appropriate preparations, and have secured Small Child into her vibrating chair, which generally gives me an hour of hands free time. More than enough to wash this beast, and then attend to Small Child before moving into the drying stages.

Of course Small Child waited until I was up to my elbows in shampoo before announcing to the world that she had not been fed in six months at least. Obviously she was starving and unloved, and needed her elevenses forthwith.

There is a time and a place for abandoning a dog of Grandma Kaegen's stature. Mid way through her bath is not it. Resigned to her fate, she lay down, not before giving me side eye of such proportions that I shall sleep with one eye open.

DAY The Sixty First (Or, I Don't Know Which Is Worse, Jabs Or Paisley. Either Way, I'm Not Popular.)

Gentle reader, today has come as a bit of a shock to Small Child. Today was jab day.

Now, having watched our friends go through this has left us less than enamoured by the idea. It does not seem like something one would do for fun. Nevertheless, it must be done.

Small Child and I attended, and much to her delight, there were cuddles aplenty, and we got to play a whole new version of Naked Baby Roulette with the Health Visitor (For those of you keeping score, it's now Small Child 3 Mummy 4) while being weighed and measured.

Then we saw the Dr. Small Child quite enjoyed the light being shone in her eyes, and thought the stethoscope was just a fancy version of my necklace. She bestowed smiles on all who approached, even if they were holding needles.

Gentle reader, in the eight weeks Small Child has been on this planet, she has not fully exercised her lungs. We had not fully appreciated her vocal range. Let me tell you, after being stabbed in each leg at the same time, nobody in the vicinity has any doubt about her lung capacity. For a full twenty seconds she let us know how unhappy she was. Then, silence. The side eye was impressive. I knew I hadn't heard the end of this.

We drove home in ominous silence. Daddy came home and inspected Small Child's war wounds in the form of two plasters. Mummy foolishly decided to remove them. Apparently this was just as painful as the injections. Either that, or she wished to include Daddy in the category of those whom she has deafened today. We were treated to another 20 second rendition, with an equally abrupt ending. It seems that it is too much effort to cry for longer.

As we speak, Small Child sleeps. I fear we have not yet seen the extent of her displeasure. I mean, not only did I take her to be stabbed by complete strangers, I also made her wear paisley. I shall pay for this day, either in this life or the next.

Pray for my soul.

DAY The Sixty Second (Or, One Does Have To Question My Sanity)

Gentle reader, in my infinite wisdom, pre Small Child's arrival, I decided to enter a dog show or two. Ones that would involve a little travel. Why is this news you ask? This is nothing very out of the way for me.

Well when I say one or two, what I actually mean is five. In six days. Four of which are back to back in two days. And by a little travel, I mean in Scotland.

Gentle reader, I know that at this, your ears have pricked, and you have sat forward eagerly. This is more like it. This sort of behaviour is what you have come to expect from me.

I shall start with last night. Did Small Child sleep well following her jabs? Did she hell. We required calpol at 6am. This of course knocked her sparko, and we had to wake her up in time to leave.

The journey. An eight hour trip you say? How hard can that be? Daddy was delighted Small Child was sleeping for three hours at a time while we drove. Well he was. Until I pointed out that an eight hour nap in the day was basically Small Child's way of giving us the finger tonight. Which would be fine, except for the first time, she is sharing a room with us for a week.

The arrival. I had the good foresight to enrol my parents in this mad scheme, and they were present and correct when we reached our destination. I unloaded Small Child into her grandmother's arms and set about freeing the hounds. Daddy unloaded the car with the speed of a toddler searching for Christmas presents in a cupboard. I continued to unload the hounds.

Gentle reader, I have missed one vital point. While we may have four adults on this trip, we also have seven dogs.

Why do I do this to myself?

DAY The Sixty Third (Or, If You're Making Your Debut, Do It In Style)

Gentle reader, today saw Small Child attend not only her second dog show, but also the first one where she was significantly smaller than most of the entries on Day One.

It's Scotland. It's cold. It's wet. It's like being in Wales, just further north. Thankfully we were inside. Small Child and I were glad to note that we were inside for both days. Both days were filled with the adoration she has come to expect as her right, and I feel that she would have been less charming and delightful in the rain. To be fair, so would I.

Now, those of you with puppies, you know that at eight weeks, we as breeders, pass the little delights on. Apparently you don't do this with the two legged varieties, they require a little longer (who knew?). Knowing this, it seems appropriate that Small Child is inducted into our world as soon as possible, to allow the madness to get a firm grip. To this end, she entered the ring at the tender age of 9 weeks. It seems rather incongruous that she left it as Best Veteran. I know these dog shows can run on a bit, but that's taking the mick.

Gentle reader, she was of course rewarded for such an achievement. While Huzzah had his rosette, Small Child had a new play mat. OK, so it was bought from a stall at a dog show, and my dogs may have four in the same style and from the same place. OK, so I bought Small Child a dog bed, did you expect any less?

It's got unicorns on it. What else was I supposed to do?

DAY The Sixty Fourth (Or, That Was A Spectacular UpChuck For One So Small)

Gentle reader, we have reached the age of 9 whole weeks with only two VomitGates, both of which I have related to you in full. Buckle up. This one is a doozy.

I present to you, VomitGate Chapter Three: How To Make Milk Come Out Of Your Nose At Lunch.

We have discussed in the past Small Child's ability to pick her moment. This again was a masterpiece of timing. Having waited for everyone to be somewhat occupied with lunch, she decided that the time was ripe to have hers in reverse. While in a vibrating bouncy chair. Surpassing both her previous attempts, she not only managed to cover herself, but said chair and the surrounding floor. Daddy's foot narrowly escaped involvement, more by luck than judgment.

Leaving Daddy to deal with the aftermath, Small Child and I decamped upstairs. Of course, what you want when dealing with a vomit covered, yowling Small Child, is for your cottage to have a total and utter lack of bathtubs.

Gentle reader, have you ever wrestled an oil covered octopus, in the rain, while being deafened by an industrial drill in a confined space? If you have, you have some idea of what it is like to introduce Small Child to her first impromptu shower. To her credit, she stopped yelling as soon as she got wet. That's when the wiggling started. This takes Naked Baby Is A Dangerous Game to whole new heights. This round was honours even. We came to an agreement. Nobody wees. Nobody gets dropped. Everybody gets wet. It was a good solution.

This of course exhausted her. She then spent the afternoon sound asleep. Not that I'm jealous or anything.

DAY The Sixty Fifth (Or, Well Thanks Scotland, You Broke My Baby)

Gentle reader, we have not long returned from the North. We have been home long enough to dry out, unpack and reflect on our life choices. Some have questioned if I have recently joined the ranks of the insane. While I admit that those are indeed my people, I can also confirm that insanity is not a new destination for me. That ship sailed a long time ago.

Anyhow. You recall how we rejoiced at Small Child's travelling abilities? How she took after her father with the enviable ability to pass out at the drop of a hat, and remain so for prolonged periods? Well Scotland has done a job on us, that's for sure.

For the first time, Small Child slept in the same room as us. She has shamelessly taken advantage of this. If we move, she is up. Having returned to what passes for normal in this house, she has decided that over three hours sleep, where it does not involve some form of contact with mummy or daddy, is not on the agenda. Daytime napping? That's fantastic. If mummy is holding her. Bedtime? What a good joke that is.

Gentle reader, I am on the verge of putting her in the sideboard and letting Zee parent her for a while. She keeps telling me she could do a better job, maybe now is the right time to prove it.

DAY The Sixty Sixth (Or, The Day I Oiled My Baby)

Gentle reader, today we undertook baby massage lessons. This is something I have heard people swear by for relaxing and calming their babies. Well we all know that if Small Child was any more chilled, she'd be in the freezer aisle, but nevertheless we went for it.

Upon arrival, we were presented with a little pot of oil. Looking around the room, we saw the others carefully removing their own pots, handling them as carefully as if it were liquid gold. Noting this, I felt as if we were being initiated into something special. We alone were to be trusted with this magic potion.

Using it sparingly, we rubbed, glided, and generally relaxed these babies. Small Child was highly receptive to such ministrations, accepting them as her right, and another level of tribute. Throughout the proceedings I marvelled at the smoothness the magic oil leant to her skin and my hands. The smell however was elusively familiar. I couldn't place it. Where could I have possibly come into contact with this sacred liquid before? Feeling brave, and ready to sign the official baby massage secrets act, I posed the question I knew you would all be asking. What was this witchcraft?

Gentle reader, the answer will shake you to your very soul.

It was vegetable oil. Break out the frying pan, she's ready to be cooked.

DAY The Sixty Seventh (Or Time To Get Wet Kid)

Gentle reader, today we dunked Small Child. It seemed like a good idea at the time, and from her comments on the situation, this sentiment was shared for the most part.

With all due ceremony, we undressed her, attached a swim nappy and a swimming costume, and approached the water. Some stray passer by prepared themselves to catch her expression upon entering the pool for the first time. Would she be shocked? Would she smile? Cry? We braced ourselves for any and all of these reactions.

Gentle reader, as always, Small Child took great, and unsmiling delight in thwarting all our expectations. She took to it like the proverbial duck, and her expression did not alter a jot.

After some swishing, whooshing and general paddling, she deigned to chatter to us both, perhaps telling us that we weren't moving fast enough. Or to stop taking damn photographs and play pass the baby.

In hindsight, hiring the pool may not have been our brightest move. This child acts more like Hope every day, and has a distinct dislike of peasants. We may be pandering to this. How will she cope when faced with public swimming? Thankfully I have had the foresight to book the pool again, and do not have to worry about this yet. And I shall enlist the help of Grandma when I do.

The one downside to dunking? It comes with devil's work afterwards. The look of outrage when I produced the moisturiser will live with me forever. I was only mildly forgiven when I accompanied it with massage. It was no sacred vegetable oil, but it did the trick.

Gentle reader, as I speak, Small Child enters her Seventh hour of sleep. I dare not speak to soon, but has swimming fixed what Scotland broke? I dare not question this aloud in case she hears me. Daddy is also sleeping peacefully post paddling. Equally I dare not mention this out loud as I may yet smother him with a pillow. I am awake. Again.

DAY The Sixty Eighth (Or It's My Tummy Time And I'll Cry If I Want To)

Gentle reader, as you know Small Child is not exactly backwards in coming forwards when it comes to giving her opinion of things. It is entirely possible that she takes after her mother in such matters. Hungry? We have a cry for that. Done a big wee? We can definitely let the neighbours know if we need to. Want to sit up and look around? We are more than capable of requesting this loudly. You catch my drift.

And so to tummy time.

Small Child has recently decided that this is not for her. Why should she have to work for her view? Even the baby in the mirror seems unimpressed. It joins in with the chorus, which only adds to her need to be the loudest voice in the room. Under normal circumstances the addition of Brother Gatties is enough to ensure a return to a somewhat happier state. Not today. Today, tummy time ranked alongside moisturiser as the devil's work. The thought of convincing her that we need to do twenty minutes a day of this was enough to turn me to drink.

Gentle reader, tummy time in this house is not for the faint of heart. It's not for those who want to remain of good hearing either.

DAY The Sixty Ninth (Or, Welcome To IKEA, It's A Way Of Life)

Gentle reader, finding ourselves adrift on Cardiff, with little else to do for several hours, we decided to initiate Small Child into the world that is IKEA.

Now, I can feel half of you shudder, whilst the other half rejoice. Let me tell you, we did not take this decision lightly. Keeping ourselves occupied with a definite plan is a far cheaper way to spend a Sunday. For those of you who are not acquainted with our past, you would not be aware that we accidently bought a bus on a previous trip. Or that the following week, we bought a small tank. Both fairly impulsive purchases, enough to send our bank manager into early retirement. So you see, it is essential that we amuse ourselves, to prevent this happening again.

That, and we had already spent an unhealthy amount on a mattress.

Anyhow.

IKEA, as you know, is not for the faint hearted. For starters, you have to walk the equivalent of the London Marathon, just to get round. Throw in a group of people who can't follow directional arrows, and a layout Pan's labyrinth would be proud of, and you get the general idea.

Refusing to be side-tracked into buying a wardrobe, we got halfway without any major mishap. Reaching the children's section, Austin successfully managed to prevent me buying Small Child a rocking chair of her own. Well, this time anyway.

In grown up fashion, we discussed highchairs, and managed to avoid buying one. We did however buy Small Child a new toy.

Of course it came with instructions. Yes, I did manage to get it right. The second time. I feel it would be helpful if they included in said instructions, a list of Swedish swear words. It would only be appropriate.

Daddy laughed, and almost fell victim to being kneecapped by the play gym. In my defence, I was holding the instructions upside down. They made about as much sense either way up. And as said toy has not yet decapitated Small Child, I'm calling it a win.

DAY The Seventieth (Or, The Day We Met Up With The Almost Twin)

Gentle reader, life is full of coincidence. Some of them are meaningless everyday garden variety coincidence. Then we have Small Child Style coincidence.

Today we met up with Small Child's Almost Twin. Bear with me, and I shall reveal all.

While Small Child was merely a passenger, and I still had stomach muscles to speak of, I started a new job. In under a week I had joined forces with another loon, who was also preparing to disrupt her quiet and ordered existence with her own passenger. She too had just started the same role. Upon further examination, we discover that we are due to offload said passengers within a week of each other. Both via the sunroof method.

Weird no?

Jokingly we discussed how amusing it would be to produce these mini dictators on the same day. As it turns out, they were only 48 hours apart in the end. They appear to have some form of telepathic communication system, which concerns us, as we live over 100 miles apart and have never met.

Until now. I'm not sure which is more impressive. The Almost Twin sleeping through the whole thing, or Small Child's side eye. It's either that, or the fact Daddy had to check that I was in fact holding a different baby.

DAY The Seventy First (Or, The Day We Confirmed I Really Do Lack Stomach Muscles)

Gentle reader, you may recall that some time ago I booked Self and Small Child into exercise classes. Well today was the day we finally took part.

My first achievement was finding a sports bra that would successfully prevent me from giving me a spectacular black eye. This was no mean feat, as since I last exercised with any vigour, I appear to have developed the support needs of a small country.

My second achievement was actually getting into lycra. I know. It's a work out of its own, and that sports bra really showed it's worth while I contorted various parts of my body.

Thirdly, we actually attended said class. We wiggled. We jiggled. We waved babies in the air. Gentle reader, I have never in my life been more terrified that I will be thrown up on. There is something both hilarious and worrying about chest pressing your baby. Squatting is bad enough, but squatting while re-enacting the opening scenes from the Lion King? At least Rafiki only had to lift him up once.

Finally, and probably my greatest achievement, I did not die. This was not through lack of trying. If you have ever been foolish enough to run a mile while balancing a plate of jelly on a small boulder, strapped to your front, you have a good idea of what it feels like to do cardio while wearing a baby.

Probably the most concerning thing, is that I have agreed to return next week for further torture. I have yet to inform my quads of this. It has struck me that Small Child, having just put away a significant amount of food, will be heavier by then.

 Pray for me. Not for my soul this time, that will survive. My knees however, they need all the help they can get.

DAY The Seventy Second (Or, Who The Hell Thought Baby Clothes That Can't Be Tumble Dried Was Ever A Good Idea?)

Gentle reader, when first we knew that Small Child was on her way, we decided to buy essential domestic appliances. A steriliser was one. A tumble drier was another.

The day we finally purchased said dryer was a momentous one. This was Adulting. It became our pride and joy. This was going to save us during the long, cold and wet winter months. Now it seemed that replacing the heater drying rack was not essential, and we even promised ourselves that we wouldn't mind having to nip to the shed in the cold or rain to load or unload this magnificent beast.

Yesterday I decided that, having managed two loads of laundry, and totally forgetting that we owned said tumble drier after the first load, it was time for it to start fully earning it's keep. Load Two contained a large number of Small Child's outfits. From dresses to leggings and jammies, this was a good cross section of her rather impressive wardrobe.

A quick glance at a few labels strengthened my resolve. That happy symbol, which for years I had ignored, shone from her clothes like a beacon. I was soon flinging clothing from washer to basket with gay abandon.

Gentle reader, things were going too well.

Have you ever been cruising down the motorway at 60mph, and then accidentally changed gear down to second, causing your engine to try and leap out of the bonnet in a rather ugly fashion? This felt similar. I was clutching a pair of jammies that quite clearly stated Do Not Tumble Dry. What was this madness? Did the manufacturers have an off day? Did they forget that this particular item of clothing was aimed at an audience that dribbles and throws up at the slightest provocation? Did they perhaps enjoy the thought of bringing some poor unsuspecting parent down to earth with a bang larger than a commercial fireworks display?

Gentle reader, I am not proud of what I called the clothing company. I am only grateful Small Child is yet to understand such wording. I can only say that going forward, these jammies will not see the light of day until Spring. I do not need such negativity in my life.

DAY The Seventy Third (Or, What A Quick Seven Hours That Was)

Gentle reader, today we reached a new milestone In Small Child's sleep. We hit the magical Seven Hour Sleep. Now, usually this kid is good for a five to six hour stretch, but we have never made it past that. Even swimming only saw us hit six before she was awake and demanding food with menaces.

Today has been no special day. We have remained dry. We were not wholly enamoured of baby massage, and flat out refused to be naked baby for any length of time. Cheerful was not a word we used with any particular conviction at times.

When Small Child decided at 3.30pm to nap, and nap hard, I feared the worst. At 4.30 I may have suggested to Daddy we were in for a rough night. She remained awake through dinner, and for jammies. Daddy held her for a good 45 minutes, but, in line with her contrary nature, she was not keen on the whole sleep thing. Knowing that his revision time was looming, Daddy handed her over.

Cue Small Child passing out within minutes.

Feeling less than optimistic, I abandoned her in the nursery, and prayed that I would at least find out who the Killer In My Village was, before she resurfaced.

Not only did I find out, I was able to put the dogs to bed, tidy up, and do the washing up. Hell, I even had twenty minutes to myself in bed before Daddy came up. Not a peep was heard from Small Child.

Gentle reader, I would very much like to tell you that, as a concerned and loving mother I woke regularly to check on Small Child. I would also like to tell you I won the Euro Millions. Both would be lies, and big ones at that. The only reason Small Child was fed at the 7 hour mark, was because she was attempting to eat her hand in her sleep. And it woke me up.

I have, lovingly, abandoned her yet again. It is four hours till getting up time. Do I dare finish this thought?

DAY The Seventy Fourth (Or, When I say dunked, I mean properly dunked)

Gentle reader, as you know, twice we have braved the wet stuff. Once with Daddy, once without. Well tonight was dunking number three. Tonight, we dunked with a difference.

Small Child has never been averse to getting wet. In fact she often encourages it. Washing her face generally comes with a beam so large it could support a house. Being splashed in the face is a particularly favourite activity. So naturally we took this as an indication that a good dunking was in order.

In fairness, it was Daddy's idea. He just lacked the courage of his convictions, in case he made her cry, and left it entirely to Mummy.

And so, I dunked. She thought floating on her back was fantastic. She even became marginally less serious for a while. Taking this as a good sign, we took the literal and metaphorical plunge. Under we went.

The look of surprise. The realisation she was under water. The beam of delight. It was adorable. So we did it again. And again. Daddy even had a go. The result was similar.

Gentle reader, we knew she was odd. This confirms our theory. The bigger the dunk, the happier the child.

One final aside, oh Gentle reader. Reusable swim nappies. They may seem like a great idea at the time, but what they don't tell you is that placing them on Small Child is like trying to fit a wetsuit to a donkey. Removal is akin to wrestling said donkey down a water slide with your eyes closed. Frankly, it was more of a workout than Tuesday. I regret many things.

DAY The Seventy Fifth (Or, What Do You Mean, Swimming Wasn't That Tiring This Time?)

Gentle reader, before yesterday's dunking, we had taken Small Child to the pool twice. Both paddles had resulted in dropping Small Child like a stone. In fact, you only had to mention bedtime, and down she went. This time, she had other ideas.

For an hour we dunked. We whooshed. We bounced up and down. Never mind Small Child, it tired us out. We may have made the mistake of being over confident in the car on the way home, suggesting that the deep silence emanating from the back of the car boded well for the night ahead.

Gentle reader, I know. We should know better.

Small Child decided that while she would make going to sleep easy on us, that a brief 5 hours was all she needed. Then it was definitely time to inhale a lot of milk. Four hours would suffice then.

Half five she decreed was time enough to start the day. I disagreed. With a rather unceremonious plonking, she ended up in bed with us. After the occasional sucker punch to the throat (ours, not hers), she discovered that sleep was a far better option when you're cuddled up with mummy and daddy. Clearly she'd been shortchanged, her cot doesn't have fluffy pillows. Imagine her indignation when she woke up back in said cot three hours later. Minus the pillows.

DAY The Seventy Sixth (Or, Let Them Eat Cake)

Gentle reader, today saw the official dunking of Small Child. Today was her christening. She had the honour of being the third generation to be dunked into the same font. She equally had the honour of wearing the same christening gown that I did. And my mother. And her mother. And her mother. In fact, every mother in this family since 1860.

I have literally never been more terrified to dress Small Child in anything. A 160 year old gown, and an 11 week old who knows her own mind. What could possibly go wrong?

We paid off the weather gods, and put 20p in the meter, so the sun shone for the day. Having thought ahead, we also had a small dress for Small Child, so I could actually relax, and people could touch her.

Afternoon tea was the focus from 3pm onwards, and there was enough cake for even my fat little soul to rejoice in, including a masterpiece made by Grandma. Small Child was a delight, as always, but the death of naps from 1pm until bedtime concerns me. So did her face when she realised we had cake. If she could have faceplanted it from a great height, she would.

Gentle reader, to save my child further cake related distress, we shall have to eat it. All of it. It will be difficult, but I feel very strongly that it is the right thing to do. Being a parent means making these tough calls. I think I'm ready.

DAY The Seventy Seventh (Or The Morning After The Night Before)

Gentle reader, I am considering branching out into giving lottery numbers. I feel I would be accurate. I certainly was over my predicted sleep for Small Child last night.

As we left the christening, there were parting calls of "She'll sleep well tonight!" and other such throw away remarks. All mentioned within the hearing of Small Child. You and I both know this never bodes well. The fact she dropped off at 7pm equally followed that feeling. She confirmed it by popping up again at half eight. Just to make sure we were still awake ourselves.

Now, I am prepared to admit that what I am about to describe as a bad night would get me lynched in most baby circles. I mean, most people would sell their partner for a clear three and half hours between each feed. Gentle reader, you forget that we are spoilt. We are used to an obliging child who knows the value of a solid fix to six hours. Three hours is hell.

I'm not sure where she gets off being tired the next morning. She demanded regular naps, and an excess of cuddles. The face she pulled when denied a cuddle because I needed to unload the washing machine was a masterpiece in emotional blackmail.

Gentle reader, when people ask me what I notice most about my child? Her beautiful eyes? That cheeky smile?

The answer is simple.

The audacity.

Day the Seventy Eighth (Or I Really Have To Watch What I'm Saying These Days)

Gentle reader, Small Child has been talking for some little time now. Her vocabulary is rather extensive. Her first word was not Mummy, or Daddy. It was, perhaps unsurprisingly, Doggy.

Doggy. I mean, it's perfectly possible that she is *somewhat* interested in her canine companions. And by that I mean she spends more time in the crate with Gatland than she does in her own cot. Mummy has been battling with the social condemnation that would come with shutting the door and leaving her to the tender mercies of Zeeva.

I digress (shocking I know).

Now, Mummy has not always been the well spoken delight she currently is. Mummy used to work in professional rugby as the only woman in the team. F*ck was used as a comma. It may surprise you to know that this is not a word found in any of the baby books. At least, not in any reputable ones. Mummy had to clean up her act, and fast.

This was going well. Whoops had been deployed in many a sticky situation. Mummy was feeling rather smug.

Then, I stubbed my toe.

Look, I tried. I did. I thought there were no little ears within the vicinity. I may have been wrong. When Daddy came home, he was somewhat confused as to why Small Child was convinced there was a duck in the house. The fact Mummy was quacking at the bedpost did not clear matters up for him.

DAY I've Lost Track (The Return To Work Looms)

Gentle reader, it has been a while since we last spoke. Rest assured that things proceed in the manner in which you suspect. Small Child thrives. I drink. Daddy sleeps.

During the passage of time since my last missive, it may interest you to know that Small Child has teeth. Two to be precise. One of which we have been aware of for some little time. One of which I became rapidly aware of when she chomped upon my unsuspecting finger by way of an affectionate greeting.

Many things we have now become aware of, that we did not know were up for debate previously. Such things as socks, and the importance of wearing them. Small Child is firmly in one camp, I in the other. Mango: Make up or breakfast? Again, opinion is divided.

Tomorrow brings an unpleasant change to our well oiled routine, as I attempt reintegration into a more adult environment. I will be expected to discuss matters with more gravity than I have of late. I feel that asking my colleagues if they need their om noms, or suggesting that our reading matter should be accompanied by animal noises may be inappropriate. A sneaking suspicion arises that mistakes will not be rectified by a swift dearie me, and a nap. Thankfully they are capable of changing their own nappies, with or without the approved nappy change song.

The past six months has been an education. I now know which parents will drink with me on playdates, how many Laithwaites deliveries it is socially acceptable to receive using the excuse of a new baby, and which delivery drivers do not judge if you answer the door in a dressing gown.

Gentle reader, pray for me. From tomorrow I shall attempt to function as an adult in public. The pros? I am working from home, with Small Child and Gatties for company.

The cons? I am working from home with Small Child and Gatties for company.

DAY The Two Hundredth And Twentieth (Or, I'm Afraid To Go Into The Bathroom Alone)

Gentle reader, it has been a while. Know that all is well in our domain. Small Child has started at Nursery and has shown that she has used her Two Hundred days on this earthwisely. She has revealed which of her Canine Companions she has chosen to emulate, and rest assured, it wasn't Zeeva.

Our daily routine is slick, and sleep is had by all. This I generally attribute to the age old practice of a soothing bedtime bath. Knowing that this was a stalwart of our nightly routine, I endeavoured to add some additional joy to the proceedings. I bought a light up unicorn.

Gentle reader, this was a mistake.

While in the bath, it delights and amuses. Small Child is enamoured of her bathtime companion and chatters to it at speed. It reciprocates with a glorious array of colours. At the end of bathtime, it is removed with no undue ceremony and placed safely on the windowsill. In theory, it shall shut off it's lightshow and rest, awaiting the return of Small Child the very next evening.

Theory is something that this Unicorn cares not for. Gentle reader, it is psychotic. As I sit here, it has been three hours since bathtime. It has been two hours twenty minutes that it has been on the windowsill. It is still flashing.

Gentle reader, it has not escaped my attention that I shall have to brave the bathroom with it flashing malevolently at me in the dead of night.

I am not that brave.

Gentle reader, here we pause. Only for a moment however. We have successfully navigated the first eighty days of parenthood. We're feeling rather good about it too. Small Child is not only alive, she is thriving. We are making this look rather easy, and we haven't murdered each other yet. I won't lie, there have been some tense moments, most notably when I discovered Daddy had eaten the last of the hobnobs and hadn't told me.

We shall now fast forward a few months. Small Child has safely navigated the winter, and has managed to avoid bankrupting us at Christmas by the finest of margins. She is now 10 months old. And walking. This is only going to get worse.

Day The Three Hundred and Fifty First (Or, She Be Walking)

Gentle reader, we have arrived at a momentous occasion. The first steps. Picture the scene. A quiet living room, filled with the rays of the setting sun. A mother sitting cross legged on the floor, a doting father watching from the sofa. Several loving canine family companions snoring in the evening light. In the middle, a Small Child, about to walk for the first time. Those first tentative, wobbly steps. The delight of the loving parents as the child totters towards their mother, little arms outstretched, reaching for a cuddle.

A beautiful picture is it not? Shame that's not how it played out in our house. Yes, there was sunshine, yes Mummy was numbing her extremities on the floor, and Daddy was reclining on the sofa. Two of the five Bearded Black Holes were indeed asleep in the late evening sun. The other three were running riot. One had a stolen sock, the other two were either planning to steal it, or raid the pantry. Small Child was indeed tottering between Mummy and Daddy, but not in search of a cuddle. She was trying to get hold of a pritt stick.

I know. I can feel the quizzical look spreading across your face as you read this. Most parents use love, sweets or favourite toys to lure their child across the floor. Not us.

The downside of course of throwing an object back and forth across the room, is that is soon attracts unwanted attention from those who are not currently engaged in the Great Sock War of 2022. A toddling child and a Giant Schnauzer chasing after the same pritt stick is a recipe for disaster. Not that this deterred us at all.

Encouraging Small Child to walk seemed like a good idea at the time. What we failed to realise that this would only serve to complicate our lives in ways in which we were not even remotely ready for. It was adorable to watch her toddle, with ever increasing confidence across the room, until I realised what she was heading for.

A loving parent I am. A parent that shares her chocolate? That's definitely not me.

Day The Three Hundredth And Sixty First (Or How Much For A Pair Of Shoes?)

Gentle reader, did you feel a somewhat unexplained shift in the earth this morning? Perhaps you were concerned there was a faint keening noise carried on the wind? If you listened hard, you heard a small thud perchance? You did? Fear not, it was not the forerunner of doom. Merely Daddy discovering how much shoes cost when you buy them from Clarks.

The additional information that we will need to buy another pair in 8 weeks caused him to emit a low moaning nose, while the saleswoman nodded sagely. The thud? That was when he realised I was actively negotiating buying a second pair because they were pretty. He recovered. Therefore I shall not show him the receipt for fear of finding him rocking in the corner for the next week. Frankly, I've been ignoring the ironing, so I don't need an extra crumpled object to step over as well.

Plus, if he freaks out over the price of navy blue patent baby shoes, what the hell will he do when she discovers Louboutin's?

DAY The Three Hundredth And Something (Or, To Steal A Book Title; Go The F*ck To Sleep)

Gentle Reader, of late we have become accustomed to a certain standard of sleeping from this Small Child. After guzzling what can only be described as the liquid volume of Belgium at 7pm, a quick story and a song or two, she nods off. A quick top up around the midnight mark and she's all set. This has led to no great relief, and has been our pattern for many a month now.

Until tonight.

As I speak, well, write, Daddy has entered the fray. Battle lines are well and truly drawn. Daddy, Mummy and Small Child are arrayed upon the side of a good night's sleep, toothypeg number nine has set up camp across no man's land.

Long has been the battle. We have called to our aid both Calpol (a tried and trusted ally), and the star projector. Toothypeg Nine has called for reinforcements in the shape of Toothypeg Ten. They are a formidable foe. I fear that we are evenly matched.

For now, silence reigns. I do not believe we have heard the last of this. We may have won the battle, but the war rages on.

Day The Three Hundredth And Sixty Fifth (Or, How Did We Get To Here?

Gentle reader, it appears that today marks one whole year of keeping alive this Small Child. You may wonder why I sound so surprised, I mean, she is basically a house plant with complicated emotions. The truth is, the only house plant we have ever managed to nature past a week was a plastic cactus. And yes, Daddy watered it faithfully on a daily basis until he was told otherwise.

Small Child has been an experience. The same sort you get when your curiosity overwhelms you and you put tin foil in the microwave. You know that at some point there will be fireworks, you're just not sure how far in they will be.

Gentle reader, I feel I must impress upon you that "winging it" is the family method of child rearing. So far, so good.

It would be remiss of me to leave out Daddy from this epistle. Daddy has been the saviour of many a nappy emergency. He is a past master of the naked baby dash to the bath, and he has never once questioned how he gets landed with the business end of this Small Child when he walks through the door after a long hard day at work. He seems unaware that I have become learned in the lore of the Evening Poo, and am quite capable of timing said handover to the opportune moment.

In short Gentle Reader, we have reached the epoch making milestone of a first birthday. There have been tears (mine), tantrums (also mine), and a sleep so deep that not even the end of the world will disturb it (Daddy's). Through all this I have a sneaking suspicion that Small Child has trained me well. I am also suspicious about exactly how fast asleep Daddy really is.

Today will see us brave a birthday party. This in itself is an achievement to rival keeping Small Child alive, as Daddy has been allowed to play with a helium tank.

For now Gentle Reader, we shall bask in the glory of keeping a small angry gammon alive for twelve whole months. We shall ignore the ever mounting collection of bottles, and worry not that the Laithwaites delivery driver knows us by name. It is all part of the process.

Happy birthday Small Child.

Day Three Hundred and Sixty Five: Additional (Or Now, Now We're Bloody Exhausted)

Gentle Reader, today saw us brave the delights of a birthday party for Small Child. There were balloons, additional small children and a demented Donkey masquerading as a unicorn cake.

In a fit of parental confusion, we felt that helium balloons was a good idea. In an even more confused state, I felt that handing a tank full of helium to Daddy was a good idea.

In my defence, he did manage to blow up most of them without mishap. He was defeated by a rogue letter. We had sailed gaily through a Happy. We were close to a full complement of letters for Birthday, however in our wanton excitement, we may have overinflated an I. We sat, silent, staring at each other. One of us reached for the sellotape, the other, the gin.

Having festooned several rooms in our house with said balloons, it seemed appropriate to add glitter. As rodeos go, you would be forgiven for thinking it was our first. You would be wrong. We just spectacularly lack the ability to link previous consequences with current actions, especially if it is sparkly.

I regret many things.

The day has passed successfully. Small Child has been adored, pampered, dare I say, spoilt. Daddy and I are broke. Both in wallet and spirit. In our kitchen sits the decapitated remains of a demented psychedelic donkey, with a glittery horn. Kind people called it a unicorn. Friends couldn't speak through their laughter.

Small Child now sleeps the sleep of those who have devoured two slices of pizza, one of quiche, a mountain of cheesy puffs, and who have buried their face into a chocolate cake. Daddy and I have collapsed in a heap clutching wine, and wondering how on earth we got this far.

DAY The Four Hundredth And Second (Or, We're Washing The Carpet Again)

Gentle Reader, you may recall from earlier missives that this Small Child can vomit in quite some spectacular fashion. If it was an Olympic sport, she would clearly be the gold medal contender. Her timing is truly superb. Her aim has pin point accuracy. And the distance splatter is a work of art.

The past ten days have been somewhat of a trial. We have used the carpet cleaner so often that our neighbours suspect we have shares in Vax. I am fairly sure that with the amount of disinfectant we have used would cause covid to eye us suspiciously while sidling past and trying not to make eye contact.

Small Child has chosen violence these last few days. She has hurled everything at us, literally and metaphorically. Daddy discovered that which Mummy already knew, that Golly and Dearie Me just aren't strong enough swear words for the occasion. And after tonight's episode of Guess What I Had For Tea While It Comes Back, even Whoops wasn't cutting it.

And Gentle Reader, when I meet the previous owners of this house I shall beat them to death with a carpet cleaner, while asking in what world cream carpets in a bedroom was a good idea.

Before any kind soul concerns themselves that Small Child is unwell, allow me to put your minds at ease. She is fine. Glorious in fact. She just has felt the need to encourage Daddy to use the carpet cleaner three times in quick succession at bedtime, just in case he has been lacking in practice.

DAY Four Hundredth And I'm So Tired I've Lost Count (Or, The One Where I Reconsider My Battle Plan)

Gentle Reader, in this tale, you may find common themes with The One Where Mummy Saw In Every Single Hour. That friends, is because it bears a close resemblance to that fateful night. Not least because Mummy did indeed see in Every. Single. Hour. Again.

We begin.

Small Child has been a delight all day, or so I am reliably informed from the wardens at the prison for feral children, of which she and her partner in crime are currently inmates. At home she was equally adorable, and generally bestowed smiles and happiness wherever she trod. Even Grandma Kaegen seemed to find joy in a rather sticky after tea hug.

Bath time came and went, with much splashing and merriment. Even the Putting On Of The Jammies went swimmingly, to coin a phrase. A bottle, a story or several, and what was this? Silence? Why yes. Daddy and I skipped, in a somewhat carefree manner in the direction of the kitchen.

If only we had known.

To our delight, Small Child remained in a state of repose until sometime around 11. This being a respectable time to decide one needs an additional bottle, she decided to let us know. Mummy was equal to this, and applied said bottle industriously. This pleased Small Child, and she soon resumed her slumber.

Until Mummy foolishly tried to make her escape.

At this, Small Child decreed that Mummy's presence in her realm was essential. On this, we disagreed. Repeatedly. At 1am, her decree was insistent, and involved Daddy's, previously unrequested involvement. At 1.30am, following a quick wardrobe change and judiciously applied dettol (other brands are available, none of which contain chloroform sadly), the battle was won.

What we did not foresee however, was round two at 5am. In some regards, it seemed like Mummy had used the waking hours between 1.30 -5am wisely, planning tactics for the next battle. Rather quickly this theory was disproven, as nobody had consulted Small Child. She was not on board.

Daddy again entered the fray, and by some combination of witchcraft and bribery, convinced Small Child that sleep was good. He then returned to the comatose state from whence he came, and remains in the Slumber of the Victor as we speak.

Mummy however, is staring at an unrepentant peanut butter covered Small Child, and reconsidering her life choices.

DAY The Four Hundredth And Something Or Other (Or, Hello 1am My Old Friend)

Gentle Reader, it appears that we are here again. Welcome. Sit down. Make yourselves comfortable, we may be here some not inconsiderable time. We sallied forth into tonight with gentle optimism. Small Child was tired. She was well fed. Her stories went down with delight. It pains me to inform you that this is where the delightful part of our evening ended.

Having redrawn the battle lines, altered the tactics, and generally decided that we would be on the winning side of the night's battle, we had again forgotten one key element. Small Child is contrary at best.

Sleep, taking one good look at the mammoth task ahead, got off the bus. It wanted no part of this drama. I wish in many ways I had also disembarked at this point. But that was not to be. I am firmly on this fairground ride.

As we speak Small Child is exercising her lung capacity to the extent that her cuddly unicorn feels like he needs ear defenders. I do not envy his up close and personal position, or the fact she has a vice like grip on his left leg.

Daddy and I have retreated, for now. We are regrouping, rethinking, and trying to figure out who could sneak past her door and downstairs for the gin with the least amount of noise. That fact only one of us would actually come back up with it has not yet been discussed.

Gentle Reader, pray for my soul. Or at least, remind me next time to bring the biscuits up before we go to bed. I might as well get some enjoyment out of this.

DAY The Four Hundredth And Another One (Or Being Your Favourite Person Is Exhausting)

Gentle Reader, as you are well aware, there is an abundance of love in our house for Small Child. You may also be aware that when Small Child loves in return, she loves hard.

She has often ranked her staff in order of preference, and while our positions on there are mobile, I have always felt that Daddy's rank was at least equal to my own. We all know that Daddy is a good egg. One of the best in fact. A Daddy of such skill and magnificence, that he knows which way a nappy goes on, and not only that, can be found in the midst of the fray, waving one in a manner that shows he would not lightly be turned from his purpose. Small Child however, appears to have a different view on this.

Lately, we have had a poorly Small Child. I hesitate to suggest she has been dramatic, but let's just say that her Oscar is in the post. As part of her stellar performance she has decided that her supporting act must be Mummy. The mere suggestion of Daddy as understudy has been rejected in no uncertain terms.

Mummy felt that sleep was an essential part of the plan, Small Child agreed. In hindsight Mummy should have made it clear that she meant in separate beds. Small Child was of the opinion that being out of headbutting range of Mummy was something she did not care to entertain. Daddy, with suspicious speed and barely concealed glee settled in to watch the football, while Mummy added depth to the groove that is well worn in the bedroom carpet.

Gentle Reader, I fear being Small Child's Favourite Person is both a delight and a trap. Daddy appears to have avoided this trap, I envy him.

DAY The Four Hundredth And Something (Or, New Year Is So Rock N Roll With A Toddler)

Gentle Reader, it is New Year's Eve. Hogmanay, the end of the Old Year, whatever you like to call it. Traditionally a time for partying and celebration. A time to stay up and usher in the new year with delight, hope and anticipation.

Or it used to be.

Gentlest of Gentle Readers, I used to stay up till well into the small hours at New Year, and leap from my bed as one refreshed at an early hour in New Year's Day. Now, I have a toddler. A toddler moreover, who feels consistent sleep is for the weak.

It is 10.30pm. I am in bed. Small Child is in bed. Daddy is also in bed. Since the advent of aforementioned Small Child, Daddy and I have discovered that we were born to be wild, but not past 10pm.

Over the festive period Small Child has discovered the delights of a two hour nap. She has also discovered that she can make up for those lost hours between midnight and 3am. Only one of us is pleased about this.

Why oh why do I have a sneaking suspicion that Small Child and I will be seeing in the New Year together, while Daddy slumbers on?

Gentle Reader, may 2023 bring you delight, joy, and less cheese than you have eaten in the last five days.

DAY The Four Hundredth And Frankly I've Lost Count (Or The One Where Mummy Has Lost Her Sense Of Humour)

Gentle Reader, it is 5.15am on a Wednesday. At least I think it's Wednesday. Time has picked up a handbasket and made its merry way south to warmer climes. In doing so, it has joined forces with sleep, who took off on a sabbatical at the end of last week.

I envy them both.

As you are well aware dear friends, this Small Child is of a somewhat dramatic persuasion. Commitment to the part is what it's all about. I for one feel sure that her nomination for Most Dramatic Baby cannot be far away. It is most likely travelling companions with Best Way To Make Mummy Worry, and Most Likely To Drive Mummy To Drink.

For the last five days, we have been firmly aboard the poorly baby bus. In usual Small Child style, when all around us were catching Strep A, we decided to have tonsillitis. After a mere 36 hours, she decided to up the ante, and claim some of the Strep A glory for herself. This was not a problem in itself, until Small Child decreed that Mummy must also have front row seats to her performance.

Gentle Reader, I am an enthusiastic supporter of this child. I am the first to proclaim her talents loudly from any available rooftop. I draw the line however, at five nights with sub 4 hours sleep. Having tried in vain to explain that I would be a far better audience if I could in fact keep my eyes open, it seems this plea has fallen on deaf ears. Tonight has been no exception.

Far be it from me to suggest that Small Child gets her dramatic leanings from my side of the family, but I am so exhausted that I could die. I just can't be bothered. It feels like too much effort, and we still have custard creams left.

Pray for me dearest friends, I fear this performance is not over yet and frankly, I'm f*cking tired.

DAY The Four Hundredth And Another One (Or Mummy V Alexa: The Rematch)

Gentle Reader, I lay before you yet another tale of malevolent technology. Technology, which at 3am, has the ability to make me come up with evermore creative swearwords. Tonight's tale revolves around some magical thing known as "whisper mode".

This mythical mode apparently enables you to converse with Alexa in the depths of the night, without waking the (hopefully) sleeping incumbent of the cot. You know, that Small Child, who can sleep though the hoover, four small hairy menaces losing the single brain cell at a pigeon, and Daddy having a shower, but who wakes if Mummy dares to breathe a little too loudly.

For months, since the Battle of the Rain Sounds, Alexa and I have had an uneasy truce. I ask, she provides. We are at a stalemate of 1:1, and neither of us wishes to break the tension first.

Until last night.

Now, to my great and unending delight, Small Child has recently taken to prolonged hours of slumber. In hindsight, I should have known this was too good to last. At 3am, my presence was requested. By 4am, we had discussed the pressing issues, of whether or not the doggies were asleep, and if Mummy was actually sleepy (newsflash, she was). It was at this point I chose, foolishly, to enlist Alexa.

Whispering in her general direction, I requested rain sounds. She whispered back, No. Well, that was the gist. I whispered again. She whispered back the Alexa version of Get Knotted. The track I requested did not exist, has never existed, and will never exist. I mean, the fact we have used it numerous times over the last 18 months notwithstanding. Six times we did this dance, sotto voce. With Alexa, seven times is the charm. As I whispered, through gritted teeth to play the f*cking rain sounds before I threw her out into actual rain, she paused, dinged and announced that she would now play rain sounds.

At. Full. Volume.

Gentle Reader, it's Alexa 2, Mummy 1. The war is far from over.

DAY The Four Hundred And Thirtieth (Or, Dog Biscuits Are A Food Group)

Gentle Reader, it has been a while. Things in our happy domestic bubble continue to be both happy and domestic. No great event has rocked our world to it's foundations, and only minor mishaps have coloured our days.

Until today.

Gentle Reader, you may be aware of a well known phrase regarding the colour of silence. Some carefree soul once decreed that it was golden. I am here to tell you that they lied.

When one has a toddler and a dog such as Gatties silence is not golden. It's suspicious.

Having introduced you to the main characters of the tale, allow me to set the scene. A Monday morning, a mother packing a nursery bag, a father upstairs getting ready for work. Numerous dogs scattered around the place....and no Small Child.

Upon realising that Small Child and indeed her partner in crime Brother Gatties were missing, I began a search. The living room was clear. The kitchen, devoid of life. The dining room, a shell. The conservatory door however, was ajar. Approaching with caution I paused to indulge in a maternal smile at the sight of Small Child sharing a quiet moment with her favourite doggy.

Gentle Reader, there is nothing as beautiful as a child sharing food with her canine companions. There is equally nothing that makes you move faster than realising that your dog is sharing his biscuits with your child.

Well, at least her teeth will be clean.

DAY The Five Hundredth And I've Officially Lost The Plot (Or The Day I Told A Bedtime Story To Some Sheep)

Gentle Reader, I have now officially lost the plot. Admittedly there has long been some debate that that particular ship had already sailed, but we now have concrete proof.

Today, while driving home from nursery, I told a bedtime story to a field of sheep.

To several sheep to be exact. Sheep that were, as decreed by Small Child, to be sleepy, and therefore in need of it.

We had already discussed the merits of the sheep having their dinner, and when requested by the dungareed dictator in the backseat, Mummy had continued driving to find more sheep, we discovered that they had adopted a more comfortable, horizontal position. From the back of the car, a small voice asked if these sheep were sleepy. Foolishly, Mummy agreed that they probably were. Small Child then asked if perhaps they needed some nap-more, to which Mummy replied that they had already had their dinner and didn't need anything else.

We drove on.

Mummy was not quick enough to notice the next field of the damn things, also lying down. From the depths of the backseat came the decree, these sheep were also sleepy. Yes dear, yes they are Mummy replied.

Silence. Ominous, considered silence from the backseat. And then...

Mummy. Tell Baas story.

A quick glance backwards showed she was in earnest. Clarifying, I ask, foolishly, do you want Mummy to tell the sheep a story?

Gentle Reader, never ask if your 18 month old wants you to tell a field of sheep a bedtime story, while you drive past them at 40 miles an hour. The answer is always yes.

Goldilocks and the Three Baas just doesn't have the same ring to it.

DAY The Five Hundredth And It's The Middle Of The Night Again (Or, Well Done Small Child, Now Pipe Down).

Gentle Reader, of late we have had some success in the realms of bedtime. Small Child has agreed that 7pm is an acceptable time for her to end the day. A bath, some milk and a bedtime story or two and she is out for the count.

She sleeps the sleep of the justly weary, the sleep of someone who has successfully triumphed over all who have stood against her and asked of her things that are below her standards. Like wearing a bib while she demolishes a chocolate mousse. Or putting shoes on without first putting them on the dog. Or, God forbid, keeping socks on for more than thirty seconds.

Until Midnight.

Midnight is party time in the world of Small Child. It has been decreed that the span between 11.30 and 3am is the ultimate time in which to perfect her many talents. Or to check that every member of the family is sleepy. The surprise element of this, is that we have no idea which two hour span has been reserved for the performance. What we do know, is that Mummy has a season ticket.

Gentle Reader, you know well how proud I am of the many achievements of this child. I have been known to accost random strangers and tell them. Lately however it seems that Small Child feels Mummy's direct praise has been lacking and needs encouragement.

And so we come to the most recent performance. Picture the scene. 2am, in the dark. A voice, innocent and sweet... "one two three four, five six seven eight nine ten". A pause. A hearty "well done" followed. Not from me. A pause, the length of a heartbeat, "un, dau, tri, pedwar, pump, chwech, saith, wyth, nawr, deg".

I was happy, proud, and ready to tell the world that my Small Child is bilingual. Another pause. "Well done" emanated from her general direction. A sentiment I concurred with. The clapping that followed tested my willpower, and I'm fairly sure dying of laughter is not the appropriate parental response to such a feat. I feel that this was a pointed performance. Mummy has been told in no uncertain terms that praise must be given, regardless of the timing of the performance. I shall endeavour to do better.

DAY The Five Hundredth And Another One I've Survived (Or, Sleep, You Really Had Me In The First Half)

Gentle Reader, of late we have been enjoying Sleep. Actual, eyes closed, in bed all night kind of sleep. And by we, I mean Mummy as well. I know, I know. Take a moment. The shock is overwhelming.

Small Child and Sleep have been not only in the same book, but on the same page, reading in unison. Not every night, I'll admit, but enough of them in a week for Mummy to actually pass as a functioning human. Much rejoicing was had by all concerned. However, before you wantonly join in, and make such carefree comments as "she's getting the Idea", or "I told you she could do it",

It. Was. A. Fluke.

Gentlest of Gentle Readers, this week Sleep had clearly skipped ahead in the book, and was barrelling through the chapters at a rapid rate of knots. Small Child was not on board with this plan.

Firstly, bedtime. Mummy and Daddy are of the opinion that once the jammies are on, bed is in the offing. It is in fact, somewhat imminent. Small Child disagrees. Of late, jammies equals party time. Mummy could have got on board with half an hour. 45 minutes at a push. You can imagine Mummy's delight at 10.45pm on a Tuesday when we are still rocketing round like Gatland on speed.

Secondly, Mummy and Daddy believe in equality in the bedroom. Not like that, behave. This is a family show. Mummy and Daddy are firm believers in the divide and conquer technique. One day Mummy supplies milk and cuddles, Daddy reads. The following night, the roles are reversed. Small Child, although previously a fan of this arrangement, has decreed no more. Mummy is the only person here qualified to supply cuddles. Daddy is relegated to the position of Reader of Bedtime Stories. Any attempt to alter these arrangements is met with objections of the most fervent order.

Finally, Small Child has decided upon the time at which Mummy would like to be woken. 3am feels appropriate to her. Mummy has objected to this most strenuously, and has had the application to alter the time back to 7am denied as being unreasonable.

We live in hope that Small Child and Sleep reconcile. Going on previous form however, Mummy does not think it will be any time soon. Mummy also feels, most strongly, that any hobnobs eaten at night do not count, and there is no proof we had hobnobs to start with.

DAY The Six Hundredth And We're Still Standing (Or, Out Of The Whole Coronation, We're Still Thinking About Those Damn Horses).

Gentle Reader, it has been a brief while since my last missive. Fear not, you have not missed any great revelations. Small Child still rules with a firm hand and a banana. Daddy still changes a nappy with some sort of Daddy-esque flare and sleeps through the night, and Mummy is still a close friend of 1am.

As some of you may have been aware, there were Royal Revels this weekend gone. There were many shiny things, and even more hats.

Now, Small Child has only been gracing this earthly plane with her presence for a mere 22 months, but she has been party to more history than you can shake a stick at. If you happen to have a stick handy that is. If not, I have several.

In the spirit of "Lets have things you can look back on", Mummy plonked self and Small Child in front of the BBC on Saturday, waved Daddy off to stand in the rain somewhere, and opened the brownies*.

*Yes, I managed to keep them all to myself. No, I will not share my secrets.

Small Child was delighted by so many hairy hats marching that she is now almost wholly convinced that the British Army is made up of several thousand Hairy Maclary's. Mummy is not brave enough to disabuse her of this notion.

However, Mummy did not realise quite how far reaching the impact of the day would be. Gentle Reader, learn from me. Do not, I repeat, do not, allow your animal obsessed Child to watch a vast quantity of horses pass by on screen while she is having her lunch.

I can feel your confusion. It's OK, embrace it. I have a toddler, confusion is how we roll.

The issue arose when Small Child realised that these horses were not in fact, also having lunch. It horrified her not a little to discover that these poor, overworked equine souls did not have a highchair, fish potatoes and peas waiting for them at the end of the Mall. Fear not, Mummy hastened to reassure her that whatever the equine equivalent of fish and peas would be waiting for them, but perhaps Mummy sounded somewhat sceptical.

She asked me again.

At midnight.

Twice.

Day The Six Hundred and Fifty First (Or, I Did Not Learn From The Duck Incident)

Gentle reader, many days have passed since Mummy had to quack at a bedpost thanks to a minor lapse in judgement. For the most part, this has been smooth sailing. There hasn't been that much quacking anyway.

Now, Mummy had a habit of picking up phrases rather quickly during her own infancy, tales of which Grandma and Grandpa have been more than happy to regale to anyone within reach. You would think that this talent for mimicry would be something I would have taken into consideration would you not? Yeah, we all know I didn't.

Small Child has been getting steadier on her feet every passing day, however she does occasionally have the tendency to stumble in a manner reminiscent of her mother at 3am during her carefree youth. As loving and supportive parents, Daddy and I have of course been there to catch and encourage her. We have at no time ever laughed and uttered the phrase "whoops, drunk again".

Gentle reader, there are two types of people in this world. Those who have lived with a toddler, and those who have not. Which of these camps the people around you fall into becomes crystal clear when your toddler stumbles and exclaims loudly, "whoops Mummy, drunk again!".

The former group don't even bother hiding their mirth. Hysterical laughter is usually heard from all corners. Sympathetic looks often follow. Once, a cup of tea was bought in solidarity.

The latter, well they tend to clutch their pearls in horror and gasp at this wanton example of terrible parenting.

I'm sure you can imagine which group provided the background noise to this revelation.

Day The Seven Hundredth And Well I Lost Count A Long Time Ago (Or, The Sleepover)

Gentle Reader, I have been remiss. We have had An Event, and I neglected to tell you. I have no excuse, other than I'm tired. I know, it came as a shock to me too.

Life has been progressing steadily for some time. Unsurprisingly, sleep and Small Child have been passing acquaintances, the four legged financial Black holes continue to sigh as if the burdens of life weigh heavy on their freeloading souls, Daddy lives to see another glorious morning, and Mummy's resemblance to a whale is so complete that she dares not go near the water in case some well meaning soul tries to roll her back in.

Anyway, I digress. We have had, as I say, An Event.

Small Child has had her first sleep over. One damp and windy Friday, Mummy gaily handed her off to the Maternal branch of the grandparents, and shut the door behind them. Not an unusual circumstance, this is a weekly occurrence after all. The difference however was that Small Child was not due back until the following day. She was in fact, testing out the hotel facilities run by her Grandparents.

Gentle Reader, I believe you know where this is heading. Knowing that Sleep was unlikely to be a travelling companion, the grandparents were duly primed. The expectation of a midnight conversation was introduced, and the local dairy farm was on standby for additional requests.

Mummy, knowing she had a night where she was not expected to wake, much less get up, woke up every hour.

Daddy enjoyed a refreshing 8 hours, similar to other nights in the last two years.

Small Child? Did Small Child sleep for twelve hours, and wake up refreshed and full of beans? Of course she did.

Yes, you read that correctly. She. Slept. I know, take a moment. Absorb this revelation. She and Sleep, firmly on the same page.

I know, I'm not impressed either.

DAY The Eight Hundredth And Frankly Who Knows (Or, Call Your Mother And Apologise).

Gentle Reader, this weekend it has rained. Daddy has been long ensconced in the back bedroom, turning it from a guest room to a Unicorn paradise for Small Child, so it has fallen to Mummy to amuse Small Child for two days.

An easy task I hear you cry, your living room looks like the store room of Smyths Toystore. You would be wrong. Not in how it looks, but in the ease with which Small Child can be amused. When we have no time to spare, she cannot be dragged from her toys. When we need to fill an hour, nothing pleases.

Knowing this, Mummy cleverly set her to work. On Saturday we made risotto, did the washing up, and loaded the washing machine. This was great fun, and Mummy thought we'd cracked it. Slave labour that was actually keen to work. Sunday, Mummy thought that she could make Sunday dinner without help. Mummy was wrong. Feeling adventurous, Mummy rashly suggested that making pineapple upside-down cakes.

Gentle reader, when you see beautiful photos of a mother tenderly cooking with her child, do not be fooled. It is not serene, happy or photogenic. Cooking with a helpful toddler is about as serene as a force ten gale. Especially one as helpful as Small Child. Not content with mixing and tasting, she decreed that ALL parts of the cake making needed overseeing by herself. This included putting the mixture into the tins. And on the cupboards. And in the washing machine.

Gentle reader, Mummy has been told many a time that she was a helpful child. Mistakenly, this was taken as a compliment.

It was not.

If you have ever been described as a helpful child, call your mother. Apologise. Buy her wine. And for crying out loud, don't make cakes near a washing machine.

Epilogue

Gentle Reader, it appears things are afoot. Not content with spending half our salaries in return for every virus under the sun every month, or providing the local Laithwaites driver with a solid income to enable him to buy a holiday home in the Bahamas, we have decided that Small Child requires a sibling.

Are you sure? I hear you cry. Sleep is already a distant memory, you disliked the 3am spider, and it is well documented that you like your wine un sticky fingered.

Gentle Reader, it is too late for all that. We are fully committed to this rash plan. Even Smaller Child shall be making their debut at the end of the year.

I mean. How bad can it be?

About the author

 Lydia is in her mid 30s, married with two adorable children under the age of three. Due to this, she has a long standing relationship with Laithwaites, and is on first name terms with the delivery driver. She is also in charge of the five bearded financial black holes with whom she and husband Austin share their home. Living deep in Mid Wales, she was 9 before she knew that raincoats could be taken off.

Printed in Great Britain
by Amazon

46231960R00097